How To Build
Marriage Unity
That Will Endure
Throughout All Eternity

How To Build Marriage Unity That Will Endure Throughout All Eternity

Author
Kevan D. Austin

iUniverse, Inc.
New York Bloomington

How to Build Marriage Unity That Will Endure Throughout All Eternity

iUniverse books may be ordered through booksellers or by contacting:

iUniverse
1663 Liberty Drive
Bloomington, IN 47403
www.iuniverse.com
1-800-Authors (1-800-288-4677)

ISBN: 978-1-4401-4410-3 (pbk)
ISBN: 978-1-4401-4412-7 (dj)
ISBN: 978-1-4401-4411-0 (ebk)

Printed in the United States of America

iUniverse rev. date: 5/21/2009

Let us oft speak kind words to each other
At home or where'er we may be;
Like the warblings of birds on the heather,
The tones will be welcome and free.
They'll gladden the heart that's repining,
Give courage and hope from above,
And where the dark clouds hide the shining,
Let in the bright sunlight of love.

[Chorus]
Oh, the kind words we give shall in memory live
And sunshine forever impart.
Kind words are sweet tones of the heart.

Like the sunbeams of morn on the mountains,
The soul they awake to good cheer;
Like the murmur of cool, pleasant fountains,
They fall in sweet cadences near.
Let's oft, then, in kindly toned voices,
Our mutual friendship renew,
Till heart meets with heart and rejoices
In friendship that ever is true.

[Chorus]
Oh, the kind words we give shall in memory live
And sunshine forever impart.
Let us oft speak kind words to each other;
Kind words are sweet tones of the heart.

(*Hymns*, No. 232)

TABLE OF CONTENTS

INTRODUCTION

It is my belief that marriage is ordained of God. Marriage should be taken very seriously and should be treated with divine respect. They way we treat our mates should reflect the divine nature in which it was intended. All too many of us get caught up with the pleasures and diversions in life and forget about one of the most important missions of why we are here. That mission is to use the time that we have been given and use it wisely to perfect ourselves. On this road to perfection we are expected to find a mate that will help complete our happiness.

All too often we find ourselves involved with challenges regarding our mate. Why is this? There is one factor that looms beneath the surface of almost all struggles that couples are having. There is one root cause behind contention, arguing, selfishness, resentment, rage and marriages splitting up. This underlying cause has not been discussed or written about until now. Most people are in denial of this one key factor that is causing so much contention and heartache in their marriage. In fact, once you read this book and use the tools provided to get rid of this nuisance, you will see improvement in all areas of your life.

Marriage can be a challenge sometimes if you are not prepared for the storm. My hope is that once you read this book and start using the tools provided that you and your mate will see a change in your quality of life. This progressive approach will help you see beyond the surface of your mate. As you learn line upon line with example after example how to use these tools, you will come forth with a change of heart. With that change of heart will come a peace that you have never felt before. You and your mate will have a oneness and a unity that you have never felt before.

Imagine, coming home at the end of the day and your mate greeting you at the door as if you had been gone for weeks. Imagine having your mate help you around the house with a cheerful heart and a big smile on their face. Imagine one of your friends stopping you and asking, "You look so happy and radiant. What are you doing that makes you look and act so happy?" Believe me; people will see your happiness once you have been able to master using the tools in this book.

To get to this point though, you and your spouse will need to understand one thing. This will take work. Yes, that's what I said, work. We have always been told to work at our marriage, right? Most of us forget the work part because we are so consumed with the marriage part and just keeping it going. Most of us just go on with life and let it happen to us. We only take action upon what is important to us at the time. We don't give any thought for how to work at a marriage until something happens, right? Then it's too late. If we are always in reactive mode when working at our marriage, then how are we to advance and get better at it? Yes, there is work involved. The good news is that as you work at it, it will become easier as you go along. Each little hill you climb will get you closer to the top. The top is where you want to be. This is how you do it.

It is imperative that you both read this book together. This book is a couple's manual to success. It will only work partially if only one of you is reading it and implementing the tools. This is a totally interactive book where both of you will need to participate to make positive things happen in your marriage. You need to work together to accomplish your goal to be a celestial couple. You can't have exaltation in the celestial kingdom and enjoy the fullness of it's blessings by yourself can you? That's why you absolutely need to read and work together on this. You can only do so much on your own at getting rid of the underlying influence that would divide you and your mate. Together you will be invincible.

It is my prayer that you and your mate will take what I have written and apply it to your daily lives. Incorporate it into your daily routine. When issues or moments come up, deal with them and don't sweep them under the rug. Act upon the moments and clear them up when they happen. Clear the air and start again with a clear understanding and a forgiving heart. The tools that I am anxious to provide for you are everything you will need to have heaven on earth and beyond with your marriage partner. Use them wisely and use them now. Don't wait another minute to get started as you become a great strength together.

PREFACE

My wife Linda and I were having a discussion one day about a priesthood blessing she had received three weeks earlier. In the blessing, Linda was told that she had the tools and knew what to do with them to overcome Satan's temptations. For a period of three weeks, Linda searched diligently looking for the tools she was told she had. She frequently prayed about it and started making a list. Every time she thought of something, she wrote it down. We talked about some of the tools that she had listed and began to really look at them in more detail. As we were discussing this, a heavy impression came into my mind about writing a book about these tools.

Linda and I knelt in prayer together and asked Heavenly Father if we should write about our experiences and include the tools in a book. The answer that came to me loud and clear was a resounding yes! Linda felt an impression come to her mind that Heavenly Father said, "My son and daughter that would please me." From that moment on we have been working together to find as many tools as possible to put into this book to help you the reader. Once I started writing this book, the words have flowed onto the pages like water from a pitcher. This work has flowed because of the inspiration from Heavenly Father.

I am going to make a confession right now. Some of the concepts and tools you are about to read in these pages of this book will be repeated sometimes. It may become a little redundant at times as I explain different ways to use the tools in *How To Build Marriage Unity That Will Endure Throughout All Eternity.* Just think of it as being at church. You hear the same things over and over again but from a different angle each time. The hope is that some way somehow the message will sink in. The message I want to convey here is that we are all celestial material and just need the right tools to help us get there. These tools are what we all need to use in order to prove ourselves to God that we are worthy of the celestial kingdom. By using these tools, we will not only improve ourselves, but will improve our relationship with our eternal mates and all who come in contact with us.

The chapters presented here are in no particular order. All are equally important and should be used together. This book is a compilation of our experiences and the experiences of others. Since Linda and I have been married we have never argued. When we say that to people, they take a step back and say, "Oh really. That seems unbelievable. Get real!" The reason that we have never argued is that we were utilizing the spiritual tools within these pages. We have used the tools in this book whether we realized it or not. We have experienced almost everything that we present here. Everything within these pages has been tested and used by Linda and me on a daily basis. You will find a lot of meat here and not a lot of fluff or filler. This is jam packed with real life examples of how to use these tools to solidify you and your eternal mate. To get the most out of this book, it is imperative that you read the book together and discuss it as you read. By using these tools, you will definitely experience a little heaven on earth as you become a great strength together.

1
DECISIONS AND CHOICES

Have you ever worried about the decisions you have to make? How do you make decisions? Do you blame others if your decision turns out to be the wrong one? Do you feel sometimes that you have no choice? What is the key factor in making a decision? Have you ever wondered why some people are more successful than others? Is it their ability to make decisions?

Do you know what separates successful people from those who are not as successful? It is the ability to make a decision and make it quickly. Now I am not talking just about being successful in making money, but successful in all aspects of your life. The success that I will address here is of course the success of your eternal progression with regards to you and your eternal mate.

Successful people make up their minds quickly and change their minds slowly. Unsuccessful people make up their minds slowly and change their minds quickly, if they are even able to come to a decision at all. I want you to become successful. Some people get into the habit of gathering the facts, thinking about it, mulling it over and thinking about it some more for several weeks. Then they ask their spouse about it. Then they proceed to ask their parents and their friends about it to get their opinion. Then after a long period of time they finally make a decision. Then they think about that decision wondering if it is the right one for a while. They don't act on it because they want to see what their spouse, parents or friends think about the decision. Then once they get the feedback from everyone they may change their decision based upon the new input from what others thought. Then they think about that for a while. They don't want to fail at this particular thing so they really study it out some more. Uggggg!

This kind of thinking will get you nowhere fast! The point of all the analysis is to come up with a decision, right? Of course it is. Yes, reasonable research may be necessary but do it quickly and make the decision. God gave us a brain and the ability to make a decision. He knew we would not always make the right decision, but he also gave us the ability to correct the decision by making another decision. If the first decision doesn't work out, we can correct it. But by all means, make a decision and implement it right away!

Many decisions we could make, we don't make. These types of decisions are based on fear of the unknown. If we do not have a plan to see them come to pass, we fail to make the decision in the first place. Sometimes we have to make a decision based on what we know is right, yet we don't see a way to accomplish what we have decided. The key here is to decide first. Your desire to fulfill that decision will help you find the way to accomplish it. Sometimes you must rely on the Lord to help you accomplish your desire.

President John F. Kennedy made a decision. He said that we would put a man on the moon and return him safely to earth before the end of the decade. This had never been done before. Do you think he had any idea of how he was going to do that? He only knew that a decision had to be made and somehow it would be done. Were there problems and setbacks along the way? Of course there were. Did they make perfect decisions every time about all the things that were necessary to do this? Not hardly. Everything was trial and error. Did he accomplish it? Of course he did. This was because a decision had been made and they set out to accomplish it. They stuck with it.

So, don't get stuck in paralysis of analysis. Don't get stuck on stuff like: do it or don't do it, tell them or don't tell them, go to work or call in sick, buy it or don't buy it, quit or stay, etc. Make the decision and implement the action. Then stick to the action until it works. If you need to make some adjustments, then do it and keep at it. Remember, once you make a decision and it is not quite right, you can always make a new decision to correct it.

Making a Wrong Decision May Benefit You

Some people worry so much about failing if they make the wrong decision. Well think about this. If you make a wrong decision about something and then find out that it is wrong, you have just eliminated one thing that doesn't work. Now you try something else until it does work. Each *failure* brings you closer to what does work, doesn't it? This life is all for our experience. And by the way, each thing that doesn't work does not make you a failure. The only thing that makes you a failure is if you quit. Quitting is a decision, a decision to fail. Also likewise, if you make no decision, you decide to fail. Make no mistake about it, making no decision is a decision also. You have got to make a decision on the knowledge you have at the time. So make that decision and press forward with it.

We all know about the great invention of the light bulb. This is a classic story of decision and failure. Edison made the decision that he would invent the light bulb. Edison *failed* over a thousand times in trying to perfect the light bulb. He tried and tried until he finally came up with the solution. He was persistent and had to fail over a thousand times before he saw the light! He kept failing until he got it right. He had made the decision that he would make it work and made adjustments until it did. This is what we should do as well. We should make the decision quickly and be persistent at achieving what we have decided to do.

Decisions About Your Mate

Now that you have decided to make your decisions quickly and carry them out right away, we need to talk about the decisions that you need to make concerning your eternal mate. If you have been married or sealed together in the temple, you have obviously made certain commitments. In my experience, most couples take on these commitments and truly want to honor them but have trouble doing so. It is in small ways that Satan works his way into our lives to destroy the sanctity of this marriage or sealing. Most of us go on about our lives thinking, "Of course I love my eternal companion and will do everything I can to preserve our marriage." But do you *really* have a game plan to make that a reality? Do you have the tools to *seal* the two of you together? Are you *working* at it? My guess is that you are flying by the seat of your pants. Am I right?

There are no manuals for your particular marriage that includes specifics based on your personalities. Yet you have embarked on this journey together to who knows where, right? You have made a decision to become a celestial couple and have no real game plan to keep it all together. For this reason I have brought forth the tools in this book. The tools in this book will help you far more than you will comprehend. It will be far reaching in all of your relationships and especially with your eternal mate. If practiced on a daily basis you will have a little heaven on earth. I am experiencing it right now and so can you.

My point is that from this point forward you are being presented with decisions that will affect your life. As you read this book you will either say yes, this will work for me or you will say no. Either way it is your decision. All I ask is that you make a decision as you read. If you want your life to change for the better, you will heed what is written within these pages. I do not want you to read this book and say, "Oh that's nice." put it down and forget about it. This is a working manual that will help you to succeed as an eternal couple. The principles herein are practical and actually used and have facilitated happy marriages. Do not take them lightly.

Heaven On Earth

The decision I want you to make right now is do you want to have heaven on earth with your eternal companion that will carry on into the eternities? If your decision is yes, then read on. If it is no, then you might as well give this book to someone else who has said yes. If your answer is yes, then I applaud you. This is a decision that you will be grateful for.

Write this down where you can refer to it often: "I have made a decision that I will have heaven on earth in my home. I will work with my eternal mate (fill in your mates name) to overcome Satan and his tactics to split us up. We will work together in a positive manner to become a celestial couple." If this does not suit you, you may write a positive statement that is tailor made for you. Either way, you must refer to this statement or one like it every day. Some people forget their decisions over time if they don't write them down and refer to them daily. This is a tool to help you remember. You must be reminded to what end you were put on this planet. You were put here to work out your salvation. What better way than to do it by you and your spouse working together to perfect each other? You must make the decision to commit to reading this every day until it becomes habit.

You will need to think about what your goal is and work toward it every day. What you are about to learn here will take the stress off of you in your daily life. Nothing is more beautiful than to be at home where there is perfect harmony, a true sanctuary from the world.

Make the decision now to read this book more than once *with* your mate. It will work very nicely for the two of you to read together and discuss each idea presented here. Tweak it to fit your life and personalities but use the basic principles to enhance your relationship throughout your life. Teach it to your children and grandchildren. The more people that use the tools in *How To Build Marriage Unity That Will Endure Throughout All Eternity* the better the world will be.

HOW CAN I BE RESPONSIBLE FOR ALL THE CHOICES I MAKE?

Most people think they are responsible for what they have control over. I bet you do too. So, the first thing you need to do is to let go of this notion that you are perfect and it is the other person's problem. The notion that they need to take responsibility for them self may be correct, but don't expect them to be responsible. You have no control over that, right? You just admitted that you are responsible for what you have control over. Well, at last time I checked, you only have control over you. So just start thinking along those lines OK. Work on responsibility for yourself and not on other people, especially your spouse. So, now that you are focused on you, let's proceed.

You must take responsibility for your decisions of the past. You are where you are because of the sum total of the decisions you have made. You choose to live where you do. You choose the line of work that you are in. You have chosen your mate and how many kids you would have. You choose what vehicle you drive and how much the payments are. You chose what kind of dinner you had last night and what time you would wake up in the morning. Everything is a choice. From big decisions to little decisions, you made them.

Ok, I can hear what you are thinking right now. You are saying, "But what about this? And what about that?" You have come up with two or three exceptions haven't you? I don't know what you came up with so I will give you a couple of examples of my own that may satisfy you.

What if you came home from work one day and sat down to eat your dinner? Your spouse had already cooked dinner for you. It was chicken and dumplings. You chose that dinner, right? "No I didn't," you are thinking, "my spouse did." Yes, but who chose your spouse to cook? Allowing or choosing for the spouse to cook is the same. You chose them to be the cook and agree to eat what ever they cook. Of course if you don't like what they cooked you still have a choice to eat it or fix something else to eat. Life is full of choices.

If you choose to work at company X then that is your choice. It may have been the only job in town and your last choice, but you still chose to work there. It may not have seemed like a choice, but you chose to work for them or not work right? If you had several choices and job interviews with various companies and you didn't get the exact job you wanted but you accepted a job with another company, that was your choice right?

If your spouse does something that *makes* you angry because you told them a hundred times before not to do it, that is a choice. You have the choice to get angry or not don't you? Some people don't see it quite that way. Do you? Some people think that they have to get angry because the situation dictates it. This is one of Satan's lies. Satan wants you to believe that you have no control over your anger. "*You have no choice*," he wants you to believe. The spouse did this and now it's time to get angry. Well, it is not so. Angry is a choice and nice is a choice.

Choices are what have shaped your life, your happiness and sorrow. By accepting responsibility for your past allows you to free yourself from the victim mentality. If you realize and accept that you are what you are and have what you have because of the decisions you have made, then you can have a better understanding of what must be done in the future. The future is in your hands. You decide what you want to achieve and how you will get there.

Take responsibility *now!* Do not blame others for your mistakes. You were put here on this earth with the ability to make a decision. You have your free agency. You have been given the ability to choose what you want. You may not always make the right choice or decision but once you do, if it is not to your liking, you may choose again. Adjust your game plan. We all make right and wrong decisions in life and one decision you should make is not to blame others. Blaming is to say that you are not responsible and that others are controlling your life. If you feel they are controlling your life then that is your choice, isn't it?

VICTIM MENTALITY

I know first hand about the victim mentality. I was once in a marriage with a woman who I shall call Tara. Tara was in her way a very controlling individual. Things had to be done her way or she would have a fit. And boy did she let me know about it. At the time of this relationship I was not aware of the spiritual tools in this book. I could only do one thing, and that was to obey! I felt like I didn't have my free agency or choice to do what I wanted because I had to do what Tara wanted. What I didn't realize at the time was that I chose to marry her. I chose to do what she said. I chose not to confront her. I chose not to discuss this with her to get it resolved. I chose to suffer rather than to speak out to let her know how I felt. I made a number of choices concerning this situation. I had actually chosen to be a victim.

I was a victim in that I felt I had no choice. I felt I had to do what Tara wanted or she would make life miserable. I allowed myself to feel trapped in something that I felt was out of my control. I could have taken more control by discussing it with her. We could have come up with a compromise or something that would have pleased us both. If I would have taken responsibility and had the tools in this book at my disposal, I would have used the *not to be offended* tool and the, *it mattereth not* tool *(to be discussed in later chapters)* and many others to resolve this situation. You get the point.

When you act like a victim, you lose hope and feel like there is no escape and no use trying to fix anything because you have no control over it. But, by taking responsibility you do have control over yourself and you can do something about it. Don't let Satan convince you that you cannot control yourself. Don't be a victim by blaming others like, "He made me so mad that…" or "If she hadn't said …, I wouldn't have been so angry," or "If I have told you once I have told you a thousand times… and it makes me so upset." People do and say things that we don't always agree with or like. We may not be able to take responsibility for them, but we can sure take responsibility for our own actions or reactions.

By taking responsibility for your own negative actions, you think you are putting more weight onto yourself. In reality, by you admitting and taking responsibility for those negative actions, you are lifting the weight off of you. Confession has always lifted the weight off your shoulders. It's a heavy burden for you to carry all that guilt, anger, sorrow and shame. If you try to cover up your mistakes, ignore them or point the finger at someone else, you are just heaping up a lot of emotion on top of you that will crush your spirit. You know the truth. Let it go. Confess what you have done wrong and take responsibility for it. What's done is done and after you confess, your weight will be lifted. This goes for small things as well as large ones.

Today is the day for you to choose to take responsibility for your past and now for your present. The present decisions you make will determine your future. You will find that as you do this you will have more happiness in your life because you are the master of your own ship. You have the rudder in your hands to steer your own life in any direction you want. Steer your life along side your mate and may the two of you reach safe harbor in the celestial kingdom together.

The decisions and choices you make today will shape the life of your tomorrow. Make those decisions quickly based on the knowledge that you have today and move forward. Be responsible for your own thoughts, actions and reactions. Take responsibility of your past and change what needs to be changed to make your life better. Confess when you are wrong so your burdens will be lighter. You are the captain of your own ship.

THE DESIRE OF YOUR HEART

What is the desire of your heart? Do you desire to make changes in your life to make it better? Do you desire to have a celestial marriage? Do you desire to do what it takes to become a celestial couple? Is your desire strong to complete what you start or is it just strong enough to start and not complete?

Desire is one of the first things you will need in order to become the celestial couple. Desire must be strong within you so that when things get a little tough, you won't quit. What is the desire of your heart? Do you just want to get through this life in one piece and worry about the next when it comes? Do you really want to do what it takes to perfect yourself so that you know you have done your best while in mortality? These are deep questions you should ask yourself right from the start. If you think you are going to read this book and be passive about using the tools in this book, then you might as well give this book to someone else. You must be proactive in using these tools or you are wasting your time. I want you to get serious about being a celestial couple. Either you want it or you don't. It's that simple. The desire must be there.

Look at your life and ask yourself, "Do I want a little heaven on earth? Do I want to live in a world of happiness or misery? Do I just want to get through life or do I want true happiness while I am here?" If your true desire is to have a happy life while you are doing your best here on earth, I am happy for you. If you want a little heaven on earth, then I cheer for you. If you are serious about being a celestial couple, I have a special place in my heart for you. You have chosen wisely.

"Seek not for riches but for wisdom; and, behold, the mysteries of God shall be unfolded unto you, and then shall you be made rich. Behold, he that hath eternal life is rich. Verily, verily, I say unto you, even as you desire of me so it shall be done unto you; and, if you desire, you shall be the means of doing much good in this generation." (*Doctrine and Covenants,* 11: 7-8)

Seek for wisdom within these pages. Desire the good things of God and He will give it unto you. Desire to change your life for the better to be a celestial couple and God will help you. Now that you desire these things, see that you do them. Be persistent at following the wisdom within these pages.

I have gathered much information for you in this book and have presented it in a clear and understandable way. As you make the decision to study the tools herein together and put them into practice, you will find a peace that you have never felt before. You and your eternal companion will find that your love for each other will expand beyond your understanding as you apply what you learn here. Learn to make your decisions quickly and change your minds slowly. Make the decision to become a celestial couple and have the desire to complete that decision. Life is not perfect, but how you deal with it makes it perfect. When the waves of life's challenges try to capsize you, take the rudder of your ship and steer to safe harbor by first, making the decision to do what you need to do. You must desire to press forward no matter what the Adversary throws at you. Make adjustments if necessary, but stay on coarse. Keep in mind the end result you want. Take responsibility for yourself and don't point fingers to get rid of the blame. You have choices, so choose to take responsibility for yourself and make changes to yourself. Don't become a victim. You will soon learn that you can do a lot of things on your own, as you should, but when you work on them with your spouse, you will be a great strength together.

HELPFUL TOOLS IDENTIFIED
OR EXPLAINED IN THIS CHAPTER:

1. God gave us a brain, free agency and the ability to make decisions.
2. Achieve what you have decided to do and be persistent at making them a reality.
3. Write down and refer to your decision statement about working with your eternal companion to have heaven on earth every day.
4. Take responsibility for yourself and for the decisions and choices you have made in the past, present and will make in the future.
5. *Not to be offended* tool.
6. *It mattereth not* tool.
7. Confession will lift the weight off of your shoulders.
8. Desire to have a celestial marriage and have a little heaven on earth.
9. Make the decision to become a celestial couple and don't give up.
10. Seek for wisdom and persistently use it.

2
Who Are We Fighting Here Anyway?

Do you know who we are fighting? You are probably thinking, "I am not fighting anyone, unless you are talking about my kids." No, I am not talking about your family. Have you ever wondered why you react negatively the way you do? Have you asked yourself why you have such angry feelings sometimes? Have you wondered why certain negative thoughts enter your mind suddenly? Have you ever reacted to something in a negative way and thought to yourself, "Why did I do that?"

Many people are under the false impression that Satan only influences other people or that it is only major events or happenings in our life when he intervenes. Life events when someone is about to be baptized or when they are about to be sealed in the temple. While these major events I am sure Satan is truly at work trying to stop such actions, many of us just don't believe that he influences us on any minor level. Either that or they just don't recognize how Satan works to influence us on a personal level. I believe that most of us go through life simply not knowing what Satan is or isn't doing. Some people believe that there is no Satan (one of Satan's biggest falsehoods that he promotes wildly).

"And behold, others he flattereth away, and telleth them there is no hell; and he saith unto them: I am

12

no devil, for there is none—and thus he whispereth in their ears, until he grasps them with his awful chains, from whence there is no deliverance." (*Book of Mormon* 2 Nephi 28: 22)

Some people are just in total denial. What they can't see can't hurt them right? Some believe that Satan only goes after more worthy or saintly people. Most just have no idea what influential power Satan has over the children of men.

It is my intention in this book that I bring to light the various ways that Satan and his demonic host are indeed focusing on every individual on this planet every minute of every hour of every day. Satan is miserable and so are one third of the heavenly hosts that were cast out for rebellion. They are very miserable because they haven't had the opportunity to gain a body like we have. They do not have the pleasures of life with a body and will never have that opportunity. They also have got nothing better to do than to work what works of evil that they can to drag as many of us down to hell with them.

How many of Satan's demons are we facing and what kind of an army are they anyway? What kind of weapons do they have? How do we fight them? What are the tools that I can use to fight against such a vast army? What tools should I use and when? These are some great questions that will be answered as we move along. Let me start out with a story to illustrate the type and size army that Satan has at his disposal.

A man was living in a country in the wilderness. He was living on a plot of land that he had inherited many years ago. One day the government of the country found him on this land and cited him in violation of one of their laws. The man was ordered to give up the land of his inheritance for the so called crime he had committed. After the man had pleaded with the government about this injustice, they said it could be resolved by only one way.

The man would have to fight in the ring against their opponent. The man agreed. Then the government said, "By the way, you will not be given any weapons to fight with, yet your opponent will have many weapons at his disposal. Also, you will be blindfolded and your opponent will not. And lastly, there will actually be seven opponents against you and not just one." The man agreed to the fight because his inheritance meant so much to him.

The day of the fight arrived. The man stepped into the ring and was blindfolded. The man did not even get a chance to see at what his opponents looked like before the blindfold was put on. The man could feel the breath of the opponents when they got close. They were carrying weapons of war. The steel and the chains from the weapons were clanging together as they walked around him. As they came closer and closer the man started to sing a popular church hymn. "The Spirit of God like a fire is burning…" The man's opponents stopped and covered up their ears. They were getting very agitated. After the song was done, the man started to quote some scriptures that he had memorized.

> "If ye will have faith in me ye shall have power to do whatsoever thing is expedient in me." (*Book of Mormon*, Moroni 7:33)

> "Inasmuch as ye are humble and faithful and call upon my name, I will give you the victory." (*Doctrine and Covenants* 104:82)

At this point the man's opponents are moaning and crying and they have backed up to the opposite side of the ring. They can't stand to hear such things. They hate it when scriptures are quoted. The man then showed forth his faith in Jesus Christ and by His power the man cast out all seven opponents. As he did so, the blindfold fell from the man's face and he could not see any of his opponents, because they were gone. The man was set free and he went back to his inheritance. The man was victorious because he used the tools that God had given him.

Now in this story, the man represented you and me. The opponents referred to is the Devil, Satan, the Devourer, the Adversary, the Son of the morning, etc. At Satan's beck and call are a numerous host of satanic beings to do his will. These satanic beings are combined together against you and me and are more horrible, vicious and devious than the opponents in the story. Yet if you even think of the seven opponents coming after you and you cannot see them because of the blindfold, this becomes an acute picture of what we are up against when Satan is involved. Keep this picture in your head and you will quickly resolve to do what you have to do to fight against and win the victory over this devious opponent.

What would have happened to the man in the story if he had not had the tools to be victorious over the seven devils? These demonic spirits would have taunted the man and toyed with him. They would have teased and tormented him trying to cause him pain and anguish. Little by little these demons would have slowly chiseled away at the man day by day, week by week, and year by year. They would keep at him day and night until he thought that it was normal to be in the ring with seven demonic spirits. The man would eventually believe that it was himself that was thinking these evil thoughts, feeling bad and wanting to hurt others. After all, he cannot see this opponent. "Is there really an opponent at all or is this the real me?" he would be thinking. The man would have felt self doubt, worry, selfishness, fear, hatred, stress, anger, resentment, lust, depression, feelings of emptiness and loneliness, etc. This is not a pretty sight.

Yet this is what most people in the world are going through because they don't recognize the fact that Satan has great influence over them. They are not aware of how Satan works and likewise are not aware that there are tools to fight him off. They are oblivious to the tempters power and influence over them. Satan does not *make* you do anything. You have your free agency so you can choose to follow him or you can choose to follow God. Satan does however have the power to influence you by whispering in your ears.

> "And behold, others he flattereth away, and telleth them there is no hell; and he saith unto them: I am no devil, for there is none—and thus he whispereth in their ears, until he grasps them with his awful chains, from whence there is no deliverance." (*Book of Mormon* 2 Nephi 28: 22)

Many people think that when it says he whispereth in their ears that this is figurative. As you read through this book, you will see how literal *whispereth in their ears* really is. Satan is knocking at your door every day with his whisperings into your ears. You have a choice either to listen and obey him or to use the tools that are contained herein to keep Satan and his demonic forces at bay. As satanic demons are knocking at your door, don't let them in. In fact, I will show you how to slam the door in their faces!

You may wonder why I used the number seven as the number of opponents against the man. It is because it has been figured by some as the number of satanic spirits per number of people that are alive today. In other words, if you just take the number of people who are alive today and add that to the number who have already lived and died, you would come up with a number. According to the U.S. Census as of March 2009, the current world population is estimated to be about 6.76 billion. Now for the time being, let's ignore those spirits that haven't even been born yet in this equation. According to the Population Reference Bureau, the number of people who have been born in this world thus far is 106.46 billion. Now, we know one third of the host of heaven followed Satan. So, simple math gives us that there must be about 53.23 billion satanic spirits to the 106.46 billion who are alive today or have lived in the past. There are approximately 6.76 billion people on the earth today. That would mean that there are about 7.9 evil spirits for every one person that is alive today (53.23 billion divided by 6.76 billion equals 7.9).

This means that there could be assigned a minimum of 7.9 satanic spirits to every man woman and child on earth today. The figure is even higher when you take into account that Satan is not allowed to tempt children under the age of accountability nor those who are not accountable.

Speaking of assigning satanic spirits, a good commander should and would assign his forces only as needed. He would not need to assign many of his forces to someone that already has been heavily entrenched in the things of the world and who enjoys doing things that are evil. Kind of like a car rolling downhill toward a cliff. It doesn't take much effort to keep the car rolling downhill towards it's destruction off the cliff. The task of assigning more of these satanic demons to a righteous person is more of what Satan intends.

> "Look at the number of devils we have around us. We have, I should say, one hundred to every man woman and child." (President Wilfred Woodruff, *Journal of Discourses*, volume 21:125-126)

All this may sound creepy and disgusting to you at this point. Satan wants you to feel uneasy about this subject. He wants you to believe there is no Satan. He wants you to think that his whisperings come from you and not him.

Something Worth Fighting For

Let's get back to the story. The land of the man's inheritance spoken of is your second estate. Your first estate was in the preexistence. The spirits that were faithful and chose Christ and the plan of free agency earned the right to be born in this world and receive a body. The second estate is here on earth after we have attained a body of flesh and blood. Something that Satan and his followers shall never have. Through righteousness and obedience we all have the opportunity to keep our second estate where glory will be added upon our heads for ever and ever.

So, the man was fighting for something. He was being righteous and obedient and exercising faith to protect his inheritance, or in other words, his second estate. Something worth fighting for don't you think? And how did he do it? How did he protect himself without weapons? He had tools. Spiritual tools. He used a few spiritual tools that you will learn more about as you read this book.

One thing is clear. You must remember that Satan is truly at battle with us every day. The battle lines have been drawn. Satan and his follower satanic forces are watching us and listening to us constantly. They are studying us 24/7 to find out what grabs our attention, what we say, what irritates us, what ways we are weak and how we interact with our family, friends, and coworkers. He knows more about us than we do. Satan is looking for any opportunity to influence us to go the wrong direction, think the wrong thing, say the wrong thing, do the wrong thing, focus our attention on the wrong thing and follow the lusts of our hearts.

Satan especially loves contention. He is the father of contention and lies. The half truths that are spun into his whisperings in our ears are so convincing. They make us feel that we are thinking these thoughts ourselves. How many times have you been somewhere and not thinking anything negative and all of a sudden this negative thought comes into your mind, Something that you know is evil or corrupt. Something comes into your mind that you would never think of doing on your own. It could be something simple like selfishness, greed or revenge. It seems so real to you and you think that the thought was yours because it is usually mingled with a half truth. That totally makes it so real to you, doesn't it? Then, once he gets this thought into your head and influences you to think real hard on that subject for a while, he adds other negative thoughts to that and builds up more negative thoughts one layer at a time. Before long, you are feeling down or angry about what you were thinking about. Maybe those negative thoughts were directed toward some person in the form of revenge or spite. These thoughts are most likely directed to a person that you are close to. Satan loves to drive wedges between family members and especially your eternal mate. His goal is to divide families. Satan is never going to have a family so he wants you to be as miserable as he is.

RECOGNIZE SATAN'S WHISPERINGS

Let me make one thing perfectly clear before I go on. Satan will whisper these negative thoughts into your ears. Then, if you take hold of that negative thought and start thinking about it, those thoughts are from you. All Satan has to do is introduce that negative thought into your mind at first. If you take hold of it and start to expand on it in your own mind, then that is when he has you. Satan will then whisper more things into your ears to get you to compound these negative thoughts. You will then be at a stage where you are more susceptible to hear more of what Satan will whisper to you. The key here is to recognize the first negative thought and to reject it before you grab hold and start thinking deeper about it. This is one of the first major tools I will be talking about as we go along.

I am going to give you an example: My wife and I are driving along laughing and joking and having fun. We both have lemonades that we have been drinking along the way. My wife Linda is down to the bottom of the lemonade and only has ice left in her cup. As we are laughing a thought comes into my head that "*When Linda tips her cup up to get some ice in her mouth I should bump her glass with my hand so as to spill the ice all over her*." Wouldn't that be so funny? What a half truth that was. It seemed so real at the time. It would just be part of the fun right? Well, it's a good thing that I stopped that thought in its tracks. Had I done what that thought had suggested it would have surely spoiled the moment if not the day. I was able to use the *recognize* tool so that I could stop the action that was suggested to me by Satan.

When I say an evil thought comes into your head, what I mean is that it could be something simple like the example above or really evil like killing someone. The negative thoughts can run the gamut. That's actually how you recognize the thought. It is negative. It may be intermingled with a half truth to make it not seem so negative, but it is still negative all the same. The real trick is to recognize the negative aspect of the thought so you can do something about it.

In the example above, what positive thing could have happened from me making Linda spill her ice onto her nice clean clothes? Maybe a laugh for a few seconds at best. I think the negative far outweighed the possibility of a short laugh. It is never appropriate to laugh at someone else's misfortune especially if you were the cause of it. Next, there could have been wet sticky ice on her clothes. She would have to be inconvenienced to go home and put on a fresh set of clothes for the day. But the worst thing was more of a mental state of mind that I would have put her in. I dare say that the laughter would have stopped immediately. Other thoughts and negative emotions would undoubtedly be present in her mind. Also, this would be a trigger point for her in the future that every time from that time forward when she would lift her cup to get the ice in her mouth, she would think of this negative moment wondering if it would happen again. There are so many other things involved in this simple example but I will not go into them for now. Suffice it to say that negative thoughts that come into your mind need to be recognized and dealt with before you say them or act upon them.

In the story of the man and the seven demons, the man who is you and me, agreed to come down on earth to get a body of flesh and blood. We agreed in the preexistence that we would allow Satan to try and test us to see if we could keep our second estate. We knew that we would not be able to see our opponent yet we still made the choice to come here. We only knew that it would be worth coming here to prove ourselves so that we could potentially inherit all that the Father hath.

Satan Influences Us Every Day

I want to illustrate with another example of how Satan influences us every day on one level or another. This is an example of his influence in a very simple way and how it could affect us in a very big way down the road. Remember, Satan is in this for the long haul. He doesn't care how long it takes to drag us down. Here a little there a little. As long as he is making progress with us by pulling us down in his direction he is happy.

Linda and I have always read various books together every night. This night was no different. As we were reading, I got interrupted by a phone call. It didn't take too long, about five minutes. Linda was waiting for me to finish. As I was on the phone call I noticed that my toe was hurting and needed to clip a toenail to fix it. I did that right after the phone call. On the way back to read with Linda, I saw that I had forgot to wipe off the stove top after dinner. I proceeded to clean up that little mess. When I was done, I also remembered that I needed to take my vitamins like I usually do after dinner. Have you been there where you just get distracted with one thing after another?

So while I was messing around with all that stuff, here was Linda who appeared to be patiently waiting for me to finish. It was probably about fifteen minutes that she waited for me. I did not know that Satan was whispering to Linda and throwing fiery darts at her while I was messing around. He whispered to her, "*He is so occupied this evening, why don't you just go into the bedroom and forget him.*" Linda was becoming real impatient. She had to restrain herself from just taking off and hiding out. The fact is that Linda and I really enjoy reading together and discussing the books that we are reading. It is one of the highlights of our day. We have disconnected the cable TV service since we enjoy reading together more than watching some mindless TV show. So, for her to want to give up the night and not read together would be so unlike her.

This thought she had we know was from Satan because this is what Satan does. He loves to interfere with what is important to a couple. He wants to separate you. This is just a simple example of a *little fiery dart* that Satan's demonic spirits will throw at you. Sometimes these demons will throw one dart after another on the same day. Sometimes these darts will be spread throughout the week. They are carefully crafted darts that connect with each other to form a bond between the previous darts to form an impression of one big dart that will eventually come crushing down on you. You know what I mean. One dart today about "*He is too busy tonight for you.*" There will be certain triggers that Satan will link this fiery dart to, like the phone call that started the interruption.

So now Satan has a reference point. Let's take the phone call for example. Now the next time we are interrupted by a phone call, Satan will build upon the first dart trigger by saying something like, "*See, he is going to be busy again for the evening. He doesn't care about you. He would rather talk on the phone. Just go in your room.*" The next time after that when the phone interrupts your time together, his statements could get even more serious. He might suggest that, "*He doesn't care about you at all. Why doesn't he just ignore the call? You should just get up and get out of the house because he doesn't want you anyway. He likes the phone better than you.*"

Satan keeps linking things together by building one statement on top of another until it seems so real to you. He starts with a half truth or even a bald face lie. Anything to stir up your emotion. Then he feeds off your emotion and builds on it to bring you into as high an emotional state as he can get you. The higher the emotional state he can get you, the better for him. The more negative emotion he can muster up in you the more influence he has over you. The more out of control he can get you the easier it is to lead you along. In this state you are like a snowball rolling downhill. If he can start you off with a little negative emotional snow rolling down from the top of the hill with just a little momentum, he is accomplishing his designs. Satan knows that as you pick up speed he can add more negative emotional snow as you roll along. As he does so and you have more negative emotion running through you it is easier for him to make stronger and stronger suggestions to you. At a certain point, Satan knows you so well that he will strike you with everything he's got to push you over the edge to say or do something that you will regret later.

Satan is a master at how he influences you because he knows you so well. If you watched someone day and night observing everything they do for years and years you would get to know that person very well, right? You would know what draws their attention, what their likes and dislikes are, how they respond to a certain situation, to who they love and despise, etc. Loaded with that kind of information, Satan and his demonic spirits that watch you day and night are devising plans to disrupt your plan of happiness. They are planning from minute to minute what to whisper to you at the exact time when they can influence you the most. They want to cause contention and strife between a husband and wife desperately.

In this case, she was able to utilize the first line of defense by recognizing her negative feelings and whisperings from Satan. She was able to stop herself from saying or doing something that would be hurtful to our relationship by using the, *this is not of me* tool. This is a tool that she used when recognizing Satan's whisperings. She new in her heart that what was being whispered to her was not from her true self. So she said to herself, "This is not of me." Then Linda used the *prayer* tool and said a silent prayer asking for help. She also had a strong desire to be with me and her love for reading and learning new things outweighed the tempters whisperings. We did get back together and continued reading together. Now we joke about this moment in continuing conversations. We will be doing something and one of us will say, "Hold on, I'll be right back." Then the other will say, "What are you going to do, make a phone call, clip your toenails and wipe the stove?" At which we both burst out laughing. We have said this several times over the ensuing months. We look back at this as a moment that has brought us a lot of laugher and has in no way been a negative situation. This was a great victory over Satan and his demonic spirits.

We have made it impossible for Satan to link this moment to something unpleasant since we have turned it into a laughing moment.

Remember who we are fighting here. It is Satan who threatens the success of our second estate. We have to be on guard and learn how he fights so that we can use the right tools to defend and conquer this foe. Your goal should be to win each battle and ultimately win the war he has waged against us. Remember that Satan and all of his demonic spirits that follow him are watching our every move 24/7. Beware of his whisperings because he is in constant battle to bring us down into captivity with him. Satan is the father of contention and lies. Choose to become aware of these negative thoughts that Satan whispers to you. Choose to recognize even the smallest of negative thoughts and get rid of them before Satan builds upon them and links them together with other negative thoughts. As you start the first step of recognizing Satan's whisperings and learn the other tools in this book, you and your eternal mate will see what great things you can accomplish as you become a great strength together.

HELPFUL TOOLS IDENTIFIED
OR EXPLAINED IN THIS CHAPTER:

1. Sing a church hymn.
2. Quote scriptures.
3. Show forth your faith in Jesus Christ and cast Satan out.
4. Choose to recognize your negative thoughts and stop them.
5. *This is not of me* tool.
6. Prayer.
7. Laughter.

3
LET'S BE HONEST HERE

You have heard that statement before haven't you? Let me be perfectly honest with you. When I hear that from someone, it makes me think, "I guess whatever they said up to this point must have been a lie, and now they want to tell the truth." Well, let me say in the beginning, "Let's be honest here." What I have said before and after this is the truth.

Everything, and I mean everything, is based on you and your spouse having true honesty between you. This tool is the foundation of your celestial marriage. Without it, nothing can be resolved perfectly. Everything hinges on this one thing. Never lie to each other. Always tell the truth and let the chips fall where they may. You are taking responsibility for you actions, remember?

As you work through things, you have to have a base and a constant. You both have to tell each other the truth no matter what. You also have to be prepared if you ask a question to hear the truth. Sometimes there are questions better left unasked. One thing you ought to be prepared for is if those types of questions are asked and answered honestly and the person asking the question gets blown away by the answer, they must let it go. You have to be non judgmental, especially in the area of past lives (past relationships or marriages). There are a lot of things that may or may not be a can of worms that could cause barriers or negative thoughts or feelings against the questioned spouse. I believe there are some things in the past that should remain in the past. Things in the present regarding your current spouse, the truth, no matter what question is asked it is imperative to reveal the answer honestly.

One of the steps in being honest with each other in all things is how you receive the honesty. Like I mentioned above, you must be non judgmental and do not condemn your spouse in any way. What ever you do, do not pass judgment and sentence the other spouse for what they say or told you what they did. Accept it with an open mind and discuss what was said or done. This is *imperative* in your relationship! Think about it. If every time you said something that your spouse didn't like and they passed judgment on you and scolded you for it, you wouldn't want to tell them anything that you knew wasn't safe, right? You would *shut down* what you said to your mate in fear of being criticized and condemned.

This is a big reason that couples have a hard time communicating. If you can't open up and say everything that is on your mind because of the possibility of condemnation, you tend to not say anything. Many things happen when this occurs. Let me illustrate.

THE JACK AND JILL SYNDROME

Jack and Jill went up the hill to fetch a pail of water. As they were coming down the hill, Jill told Jack she ate the whole apple pie she baked earlier that day. Jack jumped all over Jill and told her how terrible she was. He told her how selfish she was and other unkind stuff. Jill just shriveled up and went silent. The next time that Jack and Jill went up the hill to fetch a pail of water, Jill thought to herself, "I don't think I will tell Jack that I ate the cake I baked this morning. I'll just act like I don't know what happened to it because he was so mean to me the last time I ate the pie." When Jack and Jill got home, Jack was looking for the cake so he could eat a slice. He said, "Jill, where is the cake you baked this morning?" Jill, still thinking of the incident when she ate the pie said, "I don't know."

OK, what can you see from this example? How did Jack react when Jill told him about the pie? He acted very judgmental and condemned her. What was her reaction? She knew she was in the wrong but did the same thing again with the cake. How did Jill act then? It was to *shut down* and not tell Jack anything. She did not want to communicate in fear of his negative reaction. So, when Jack looked for the cake, he asked her about it. In fear again of retaliation, she lied about not knowing what had happened to the cake.

This is not what you want in your marriage is it? In this case if Jack had been open and listened to what Jill had to say the first time they could have worked something out. They could have discussed why Jill ate the pie in the first place. Maybe there was a reason. Maybe Jack could help her in some way to not eat the whole desert but only part of it. Maybe Jill needs to make a different desert that she doesn't like as well. Maybe Jill shouldn't even make deserts at all. If Jack had been open to discuss this issue as well as Jill, they could have found a solution before Jill ate the cake the next time.

Next, Jack caused Jill to shut down her honest communication between her and Jack. She was shut down because she did not want to be judged and criticized by Jack. So to avoid this she said nothing and then lied about it when it was discovered by Jack that the cake was missing. What was Jack going to think at that point? He is going to look around and say, "Hmmm, if the cake is missing and Jill says she doesn't know where it is, I am not sure I believe her. I don't believe her because she ate the pie last week and now the cake is missing. Hmmm, could it be that she ate the cake too?" You see how this causes Jack to mistrust Jill. Then Jack starts to think later, "If Jill is lying to me about eating this cake, what else is she lying to me about? I think I will watch her every move to see if she is lying about something else."

By Jacks mistrust and checking up on Jill constantly, Jill feels uneasy and is irritated with Jack's persistence. She starts to think Jack has a "problem" and so she shuts down totally and doesn't tell Jack anything. That way there is no checking up on anything because she doesn't even speak to Jack much. Wow! Do you see how this pattern of mistrust can ultimately spiral out of control? What a sorry situation, huh?

Now, this story is not about eating cakes and pies, is it? Do you see any cakes and pies in your life? Do you see little things that you can't be honest about with your mate because you fear the judge and an onslaught of negative criticism? This is indeed the basis for which you need to bring about change in your life in order to succeed as a celestial couple. You must be honest, not be judgmental and have unconditional love for your mate.

The biggest killer of open honest communication is when one or both of you act as judge, jury and executioner. Remove this negative reaction and seek for understanding and love of the other person. Recognize that we all have faults and are trying to overcome each of these trials that are placed in front of us. Remember to love the sinner but hate the sin.

If you have fallen into this trap of not being honest with your spouse, do something about it. Right now, have an open honest discussion about how the two of you will be honest and open with each other starting today. Forgive each other for any past lies, half truths, or omissions. What is in the past is in the past. Start fresh having faith in one another to fulfill this new and wonderful agreement. Discus about not judging one another for what they say and accept it as truth. You must have unconditional love for your mate. No matter what they say, you must love them anyway. Look past their weaknesses and love them. Remember, you are both working on yourselves and helping each other. If you can't accept the fact that your mate is not perfect, how can you expect your mate to look past your imperfections?

Don't have such high expectations of your mate that you will be disappointed. The only expectation you should have as you work together is that you both have a lot of work to do and you are both working on perfecting yourselves. In other words, expect that your mate is working on getting better at what they are working on. When they are working at something, don't expect them to be perfect at it right away. If they mess up, don't say to them, "I thought you were working on that. You aren't any better at that than you were last week." That is an unrealistic expectation. If you can help your mate in an area please do so, but don't expect that they will be perfect at it within a certain time frame. Compliment them as you see improvement. This will help reinforce their efforts to improve. Never use any negative comments because this will impede their efforts.

I Believe You

Ok, now that you have discussed that you will be honest with each other, the next step is to believe what the other person is saying. This can be hard at times because of things that have happened in the past. It can be hard to believe because of certain tone inflections in your spouse's voice. I can tell you that many times your belief in what someone says to you can be interpreted many different ways. The reason for this is because the tonality of how someone says something can be interpreted to mean different things to different people.

A lot of people tend to think the worst when someone says something with certain tonalities. My suggestion to you is this. When in doubt, ask your mate what they really meant by what they said instead of assuming something that may not be true. I have found that sometimes I have said something to Linda in a certain voice or tonality that she interpreted as something that I really didn't mean. For whatever reason, I was in a certain mood that what I said came out in a way that seemed not appropriate. Linda, being disturbed by how I said what I said, stopped and asked me what I meant by that. I was then given the opportunity to explain what I meant, which was totally different from what she thought I meant. This saved us so much time and anguish because we cleared up the miscommunication before it turned into a lengthy discussion. You know what I mean?

The reason you want to clear up any possible miscommunication is that you want to be able to believe what your mate says, right? You want to believe them in the way that they truly meant for you to hear what they were saying. You want to believe the truth rather than your version of what you thought they meant. I heard this quote many years ago that seems to go well with what I am saying right now.

> "I know you believe you understand what you think I
> said, but I am not sure you realize that what you heard
> is not what I meant." (Quote by Robert McCloskey)

This is so true with a lot of communication between a husband and wife. The art of assuming really takes its toll when trying to out think your mate. Take what your mate says and believe what they say and not what you believe the meaning is behind what they said. Don't try to read into something that may or may not be there. Take what is said at face value. If you don't quite understand what they really meant, ask them. After you ask them, believe them. Remember, you are being honest with each other and as such, you must believe what your mate is telling you.

This may be such a new concept for you that it may be a difficult practice to harness. Most of us have such a hard time with assuming what someone says and concocting the supposed meaning behind it that it may be difficult to train ourselves to ask our partner what they really meant. This is a practice that you really need to get down. It is *really* important! This is one of the keys to your success as a celestial couple. Everything from here out depends on your complete honesty with each other and then believing what has been said. Believe them as they meant to be believed. You get what I am saying here don't you? Ok, just to make it perfectly clear I will relate to you the following example.

Mike and Cindy are getting ready to go out for the evening to a big party. Mike got home a little late and is rushing around trying to get ready. He suddenly notices that Cindy changed her hair style. He thought to himself, "Cindy must have gone to the hair stylist today and changed her hair style. I like what she did with her hair." Thinking this as he is rushing to get ready, he says to Cindy, "Nice hair." Mike, thinking he has just paid Cindy a compliment, goes on about getting ready. Cindy on the other hand hears the compliment in the rushed voice of her husband as a "cut down." She hears it in the tonality as in, "Nice hair. Yeah right!" You know the tonality I am talking about. So, Cindy gets to thinking, *"Mike doesn't like my hair. He thinks it looks dumb. I don't know if I even want to go to the party with Mike and this dumb looking hairdo."* On and on Cindy is thinking negative thoughts about what Mike said not knowing that she is just assuming something that is not true. Satan is throwing in his little negative whisperings to Cindy.

The first thing that Cindy needs to do is to believe what Mike has said. Then, since she was confused by his tonality, ask him what he meant in a loving way. She should not approach Mike with an attitude by saying, "What did you mean by THAT?" She should say something like, "Do you really like my new style?" This gives Mike the opportunity to say what he really means. "Yes darling, I really like it," might be his response. This way of clarifying is the ideal way to end the miscommunication before it even starts.

I will explain more about communication in a later chapter but for now I just want you to focus on believing what your mate says. The two of you *must* make the commitment to always tell the truth no matter how bad it looks or what the consequences are. This includes no finger pointing or sugar coating anything to make you look good. This is imperative that you both do this or some of the other tools in this book will not work. As you both tell the truth to each other, you will have the confidence to believe what is being said. You will know that what your mate is telling you is true. It's ok to mess up about something and tell your spouse that you messed up. As the saying goes, the truth will set you free! It will free up your mind to say what is, instead of having to make up a story that you will have to remember later on. Eliminate these deceptions and breathe easier by being open and honest.

Satan, the father of lies wants you to be deceptive and lie a little here and there. *"It won't hurt you with a little lie here and there. No one will know,"* Satan whispers into your mind. Just remember the story of Jack and Jill and how it affected their relationship. Satan tries to get in there with just the smallest little deception. He knows that if he can get you to lie one time, he can get you to lie again. Each time it gets easier and easier for him to persuade you to go another step into the darkness until he grasps you with those awful chains from whence there is no deliverance. You get the point I am sure.

Concentrate on always telling your eternal mate the truth and believe what they say. Clarify what is not clear. Do not be the judge, jury and executioner. Be open minded, be non judgmental, love unconditionally and discuss your honest feelings with each other. If one spouse is having trouble with any one of these, help them to be stronger in overcoming their weakness. If you are helping each other you are only helping yourself. You cannot reach exaltation in the celestial kingdom by yourself. Helping your mate to overcome their weakness is being Christ like. It is easy to talk about the things you agree on and I encourage you to do so. It is more rewarding though to work through difficulties and achieve victory with a positive result. I guarantee that the more you openly communicate honestly and believe each other the more you will become a great strength together.

HELPFUL TOOLS IDENTIFIED
OR EXPLAINED IN THIS CHAPTER:

1. Tell the truth. Be honest with your mate in all things.
2. Choose to be non-judgmental with your spouse.
3. Do not condemn your mate.
4. Discuss things openly and honestly with your eternal companion.
5. Have unconditional love for your spouse.
6. Forgive each other.
7. Compliment your mate's improvement.
8. Believe your companion.
9. Do not assume anything.
10. Ask your mate for clarification. Practice asking what your spouse really means.

4
I Can't Think Positive, Can I?

A while back I went to a movie that was very interesting. It wasn't a well known movie but it had some interesting points to it. It is called *What in the Bleep Do We Know*. It was more of a documentary than a movie. But the most interesting part of the movie was where a scientist took ordinary water in containers and taped the words hate, kill, hurt and other negative words on the containers. He froze these containers and then took pictures through a microscope of the ice crystals. He then took water from the same source and taped positive words onto the containers such as love, peace, happy, etc. He froze those containers and took pictures through the microscope of those ice crystals. He compared the two sets of pictures and you know what he saw? The positive word group of ice crystals was very beautiful in design with star burst and pretty symmetrical forms. But the negative word pictures of the ice crystals looked totally different. The negative ice crystals were disorganized, fragmented and looked ugly compared to the positive word ice crystals. It was an amazing difference. The point of this story is to make you think. According to *Wikipedia* the human body is about 60 percent water in adult males and 55 percent in adult females. What really happens to our bodies on a molecular level when we think, say, writes or hears negative words like hate, kill and hurt? And what good can come to our bodies when we think, say write or hear positive words like love, peace and happiness? How does it all affect our lives and how we feel?

So how and why should we think positive? This is a great question. Have you ever thought about this? So many of us are engrained to look at what's wrong with things rather than what's right. We have been so conditioned to just accept what's right as being normal and customary. Most of us do not even think of what is good in our life. Once we get what we want, that becomes the *norm* and all we can think about is what's wrong or what we don't have. I am going to focus on situations rather than on things here. This is because situations between celestial couples are much more important and correctable.

Positively Grateful

Let me start out by saying that we should all be grateful for all that we have. Being grateful is a positive step towards eternal life. The act itself of being grateful is positive in itself. If we are not grateful, we are taking advantage of others. Giving thanks to God for all that we have is a great first step towards being positive. Look around you and be grateful for your body and all of its parts. If some parts don't work as well as others, be grateful for the parts that do work well. I guarantee that how ever bad off you think you are, there is someone that is worse off than you and they are thankful to be alive. Be thankful for your spouse, without which you could not be a celestial couple.

Look around you and see the goodness that God has given you and give thanks. Look at the positive things. Forget the negative things right now. See the beauty for what it is. We are going to look at what you can do as a celestial couple to help each other and to enhance your life through all eternity.

Many of us have had negative situations happen to us in the past. Maybe you are going through a negative situation right now. I believe these situations happen to us for a reason. They are what make us who we are. How we handle these situations develop us as individuals. We are being tried and tested to see what we will do. Things that are from

Satan are negative and things that are positive are from God. We are given our free agency to choose one or the other. What experiences will we have? Who will we follow? We are who we are because of our life's experiences. When you sum up your experiences what will you find? Will they be on the negative or positive side?

BANK YOUR ATTITUDE POSITIVELY

In a way, we are like a checkbook register. Using a checkbook register, you keep an accounting of the money in your bank account. When you deposit money you write the amount in the plus column and add this to the current balance. When you write a check, you deduct that amount from the current balance. The more money you deposit into your bank account the happier you are right? You are showing improvement in your bank account balance. That's a good thing right? No one wants to run out of money. So the more money you deposit the better.

On the other hand, as we pay our bills we have to write checks and draw out of the account we are building up. We don't feel as good about this because our account balance is now getting smaller. We are deducting money from our account and the positive balance is dwindling. No one likes to have to write more checks that withdraws more money than they have in the bank do they? That would put them in the negative and they would have to borrow money in order to pay the bills right?

Do you get where I am leading to about positive and negative balances? Of course you do. So it is with positive and negative things you think about in your life. Did you know you have an attitude bank? That's right. When you do, say or think positive things, you are adding to your attitude bank account. When you do, say or think negative things you are deducting from your attitude bank account.

Some other people, not you of course, are so negative that they are borrowing their negativity because they haven't contributed anything positive to their attitude bank in years. You know people like that don't you? These are the people that can't think of one positive thing about anything even when it is staring them in the face. You know, you can find something negative about everything in this world if you look hard enough. With these kind of people their mother could come up to them and give them a bowl of their favorite ice cream and all they can think of is that the color of the bowl she gave them should have been blue instead of green. They might say that there should have been more ice cream in the bowl and that it's now 8 pm and she should have given it to you by 7:15 p.m. because that's when you always eat your ice cream when you are at home. The spoon was a little one and they wanted a bigger one, and on and on etc. You get the point, right?

Where do you think they are borrowing the negativity? I believe they are trapped in the web Satan has cast out for them. Satan allows them to *borrow* as much negativity from him as they want. *"Sure,"* he says, *"borrow as much negative statements and feelings from me as you can. I will freely dish it out to you. I want you to be in debt to me for life!"* Your life is what he means! People feed on this borrowed negativity until they *own it*. The more they own it and allow these negative feelings into their heart, the more they get addicted to them. People who get addicted to these negative thoughts and feelings feel that they can't control themselves. Since they *own it*, they think and feel that it is *just the way they are*. When people think this, Satan has achieved his designs and he has got one more soul under his spell. Satan has dragged them down into this awful habit so that he will have more influence over them. He has convinced them that there isn't any good in the world and that they must tell everyone around them how unhappy they are and how awful everything is. Satan wants them to spread the bad news and infect other people to support the demonic army.

As negative people tell their story of woe, many others are often sucked in. You know the story. One person tells what happened to them and how bad it was and then the next person has to relate a story of what happened to them in a similar situation but it was worse. Then someone else will try to top that bad story. It is so sad the way this negative talk brings everyone down. It is sad that the more negative things you talk about, the more negative things come into your life for you to talk negatively about. It's a vicious circle.

Have you ever heard the statement you are what you eat? Well I believe you are what you think. You also attract what you think about. In other words, if you are thinking negatively all the time, you will attract negative things. If you think positively you will attract positive things. I know this to be true. Have you ever seen any real successful people who were always negative? I don't know of one. They are always positive. You may think, "Of course they are always positive, they are successful. I would be positive too if I were successful." I don't think so. It's the positive person that becomes successful. They don't become successful and then start thinking positive. It's the positive person who thinks he can do something and then does it. The negative person thinks of all the reasons he can't do something and so he doesn't. The point here is if you think you can do something or if you think you can't, you are right. It's all in the attitude and how you approach the problem or life itself!

THINK POSITIVE THOUGHTS ABOUT YOUR SPOUSE

I would like to reprint a poem that I found by an unknown author entitled Builders or Wreckers.

> I watched them tearing a building down,
> A gang of men in a busy town.
> With a ho, heave, ho and a lusty yell,
> They swung a beam and a wall fell.
> I asked the foreman, "Are these men well skilled?
> Like the men you'd hire if you had to build?"
> He laughed as he replied, "No, indeed.
> Just common labor is all I need.
> I can easily wreck in a day or two
> What builders have taken years to do."
> I asked myself as I went away
> Which of those roles have I tried to play?
> Am I a builder who works with care,
> Measuring life by a rule and square?
> Or am I a wrecker who walks the town
> Content with the labor of tearing down?

Why is it that many of us find it easier to be a wrecker instead of a builder? We should seek to build each other up and not be so critical and find errors and point fingers to tear each other down. Life would be so much better if we were all builders. Don't you agree? Think about this poem and your spouse at the same time. Be a builder.

The key here in being a builder is to think positive and your positive actions will follow. I bring this up because as you are with your spouse, you must think positive things about them *all* the time. I know what you are thinking, "How can you think positive thoughts about your spouse all the time?" You are thinking, "If my spouse says or does something to offend me or make me angry, how can I think positive about them?" OK, grant you, this will take some effort on your part.

TRUE SELF VERSES INFLUENCED SELF

To do this the easiest way, I have devised a way of thinking about my wife Linda. I know her well enough that I know her true self and what she wants out of life. I know how she acts when she is happy and under her own control. I know that she loves me and cares for me and wants to be a queen in the eternities. These are just some of the positive things that I keep in my mind about her. Part two of what I know about Linda is that she has a few weak areas that Satan is working on to bring her down. I know these weaknesses and know how Satan influences her to become reactive in certain ways. The reason I know this is because we are focused on each other and have gone through enough experiences for us to know where Satan is hitting her hardest. Through practice and many conversations with your spouse, you will get to this level too.

I take this knowledge about my wife Linda into account when a situation should arise. Knowing that she would never hurt me intentionally, I look at her in two different ways when she becomes a *challenge*. For example, there have been times that she has said something that could really offend me deeply. I now recognize when she has given into demonic suggestions and is now playing out those thoughts and actions that have influenced her. She gives me several signs unknowingly that help me realize that Satan has got hold of her.

In other chapters I will get into how you can recognize these signs in your spouse. For now I will give you three basic steps that I use that you will need to know. I will expand on these steps in a later chapter.

The first step for me is to recognize that the *true Linda* is not there. I can see that she is heavily influenced by Satan. Therefore, right off the bat, I know that what she is saying or doing is not of her, it is from Satan. Therefore, at this point, I might as well be talking to Satan. So you see, what I have done is split what is happening into two parts, Satan's influence and the *true Linda*. I realize that what is coming out of her mouth or what action she is taking is not really her. My real battle is with Satan.

Step number two is that you must not take it personally and choose not to become offended. This is a big step but a crucial one. No matter what your spouse says, you must realize it is from Satan and not your spouse. You have to realize that Satan wants you to respond negatively. If you do respond negatively you are falling into his trap. If you ignore the negative comments from Satan and use the spiritual tools in this book to get rid of his demonic influence, you will save the day. Work on yourself first. Say to yourself, "I choose not to be offended." Stay calm as if someone had just said something nice to you. No matter what is said to you, do not take it personally. No matter how personal the attack, do not take it personally. Satan wants you to, but do not fall into that trap. I cannot emphasize this enough. Take a stand to not be offended and do not take anything personally that is said to you at this time. Once you are under control, proceed to the next step

Step three is to use the tools provided in this book. I use a number of tools like, not being offended, don't take it personally, cast Satan out and or the stop stop stop tool. Here's how it works.

One tool that we use most often is a tool that Linda and I have set up ahead of time. We use this when one of us is obviously under Satan's influence the other will put up their hand and say, "Stop, stop, stop." This being set up by us ahead of time is a pattern interrupt so that we can recognize what the other person sees in us. That gives us a chance to collect our thoughts and see where we are and try to correct it with the help of the other spouse.

We may use this tool and or several tools together or in sequence to help the spouse under Satan's influence get out of this mode. Another tool we like to use is the cast Satan out tool. As you read on you will pick up more and more tools to help you in various situations.

So, separating Satan's influence from the *true Linda* has helped me to think positive thoughts toward Linda as I focus my attention on helping her to recognize she is under Satan's influence. Once she recognizes this, it is much easier to rid those evil demons influence on her. Sometimes it has taken the two of us to get rid of the father of contention. This is why you must work together in this battle with Satan.

Here is another example of one of Satan's tactics as he tries to influence you to think negatively. He doesn't want you to think positive at all. Linda and I are collaborating on writing this book together. Our discussions and experiences have brought wisdom onto these pages. After such discussions I write down what we have talked about. As I have been writing this book, we will pause and read what I have written. I had just finished writing a particular chapter and Linda was reading it. She looked up at me with tears in her eyes and said to me, "This book is just so touching. It is deep and yet so down to earth. Your book means so much to me." At that moment, I had a feeling come over me. It was the fiery darts from Satan that put this thought into my head and I did not recognize it fast enough. I looked upset and said in a stern voice, "Why would you say that?" Linda, recognizing that my demeanor had changed and immediately put her hand up with her palm facing me and said, "Stop stop stop. How could you say that differently? I just complimented you about your book and you just slammed me." I stopped for a minute and started to think. Linda had just helped me to recognize Satan's influence on me. As I started to think about how to rephrase that comment, Linda recognized that the upset look on my face disappeared and was replaced by a smile. The tense feeling I was experiencing as I said, "Why would you say that?" was leaving me as I thought of how to rephrase that comment positively. I was now in a pleasant mode in which I began conversing with Linda. After Linda used the *how could you say that differently* tool, I pleasantly said, "Thank you for stopping me and helping me to get out of that negative mode and thank you for the compliments." I continued to think positive thoughts about Linda after she corrected me. This is a must!

When your mate helps you to see what you are not seeing in yourself, you must think positive thoughts about them. Appreciate what they are doing for you by helping you to be positive. If you are always being helped by your mate in a positive way to improve yourself then be happy about it. Thank your mate for the help. As you help each other you are only helping yourself because the two of you are becoming one. You are becoming one spiritually.

Satan does not want me to write this book. He is angry about it I am sure. The more people that know about his tactics and have the tools they need to fight him off and better their lives the more he is trying to destroy this work. He knows that my goal is to help as many people as I can to have the heaven on earth that Linda and I are experiencing right now. Satan would like nothing more than to shut me down as fast as he can. This tactic he used was to influence me to cut down my own book and drive a wedge between Linda and me so that the book would never be published. The father of contention was still at work trying to thwart the cause of freedom from his awful chains that would bind us.

I Can See Clearly Now

Do you let little things bug you? When you see something about your mate that bugs you, do you focus on it? When you focus on the negative, you are only giving into Satan's temptations. He wants these things to *bug* you. Any time he can get under your skin and cause irritation he is more than happy to do so. I want to relate a little story that Linda related to me a couple of days a go.

Linda was driving her newly washed car down the road. As she was driving, a bug smashed her windshield. It was a small bug, but nevertheless, it made a spot on her windshield right smack in the middle of her view. As she drove, she kept looking at the spot and focusing her attention on it. It was becoming irritating. She didn't want to use the windshield wipers on it because it might smear. Also, she had just washed the car and didn't want a mess on her newly washed car. You know what I am talking about, right? Well, the more she was thinking about this bug on her windshield, the more upset she was getting. Then something happened.

She remembered about our conversation a couple days earlier when we were discussing this book. She thought to herself, "I am going to focus on the nice clear view out of the rest of my nice clean windshield and forget about that bug! There is so much more windshield to look out of around that bug." And that's what she did. As Linda looked out the nice clean windshield, not only did she see the road and the other cars on the road but she was able to see the nice beautiful sky and clouds. She saw the colorful wildflowers alongside the road and the mountains far off. She saw the nice things around her that she normally takes for granted. She could no longer see the bug on her windshield because she was looking past it. The bug that was bugging her was no longer her focus. The beauty around it was more important to focus on and enjoy.

Linda began to liken that situation to me. She thought about all the good things she knows about me. She thought of all the good times we have shared together and focused on my good qualities. She had no thoughts about anything that was irritating or that bugged her about me. As Linda said to me, "I saw the goodness, purity and strengths about you and I felt uplifted. It was like looking through different eyes. Everything brightened up and I felt uplifted, just like I went to a different world! I was focusing on the good."

What a great example for all of us. Don't let the things that bug you get under your skin. Don't focus on them. When you look at your spouse, look through the clean part of your windshield and see the good things about them. See the positive and great things that they do. Your eternal mate has some awesome qualities. Focus on those fantastic qualities that you know that they possess. Look past the imperfections and things that bug you. Look at the beauty that your mate has that you have taken for granted. Be grateful for all that your mate brings to your life. We are all beautiful in our own way. This beauty that is in front of us is more important to focus on and enjoy. Recognize it and be grateful for it. Seek the positive and you will find it. Be uplifted by it.

THE LAW OF RECIPROCITY

More about thinking positive and acting positive. There are many books that have been written on the power of positive thinking. I suggest you pick up a couple of them and read them. The power of positive thinking has got to be one of the most powerful things you can do for your own well being and for your celestial marriage. As you think positively your actions following these positive thoughts will produce positive results.

An example of this rang true for me. I have always said positive things to my wife Linda. It has always been important for me to build her up and help her to think good of herself. This is especially meaningful to me since I know that she was treated exactly the opposite when she was a child. I will say things like, "You are so smart and witty. You are so much fun. You are such a great first grade teacher. I know why the students love your class. It is because you are so fun and entertaining while you are teaching them. I love the way you do my laundry each week, etc." I have seen how these comments uplift her and make her happy. In turn, she makes such sweet and meaningful positive statements to me at various times to uplift me and make me feel good.

You can see that what you put out you get back. As the old saying goes, what goes around comes around. This happens all the time. You know what I am talking about. Your feelings are transmitted to the other person. Then they feel compelled to give back to you what you gave to them. If you give out negative argumentative comments, then that is usually what you get back. As for myself, I prefer to get back positive statements so I give them out as freely as I can. I don't just flatter my spouse with empty comments and neither should you. Give heartfelt statements that you truly feel. It's not that you should be looking for positive comments to be said back to you, I just know it will happen automatically. This is the law of reciprocity in action.

JUST KIDDING

"Danger danger," as the robot would say in the old *Lost in Space* TV show. Here is a place that Satan will try to enter and divide you as a couple. It is a pattern that I have seen time and time again. In fact in times past I had fallen victim to this demonic snare. It is when a couple is kidding around and having fun that these negative satanic suggestions are planted into your mind. Satan will whisper to you to say a certain thing that will sound funny in your mind to you, because he wants you to feel that way, but will be hurtful to your spouse, usually some dig in an area that your spouse is sensitive about. Satan is masterful at crafting a comment in your mind to get you to think it is funny. Once you have said it, suddenly you know you shouldn't have, because at that moment you knew that was an area of sensitivity for your spouse. You see your spouse gasps and is visually hurt. Satan has just scored again.

Isn't this a great example? You have been there right? You know you shouldn't have said something but now that you have, you can't take it back right? The next common thing for you to say is, "Just kidding." Yeah right! This excuse of *just kidding* has been so overused that it no longer means what it is supposed to mean. The comment still hurt the other person even when kidding around. The fact that you were just kidding doesn't make the hurt immediately go away.

I was brought up in a small town and had a group of friends that would crack all sorts of humor. Most of the so called humor was cut downs to other people. One of my friends would smile and raise his eyebrows up and down several times quickly after making a sly cut down to someone. His gesture was to say, "Just kidding." My suggestion to you would be to avoid *any* cut downs toward anybody, especially your spouse. No matter how funny you think it is. Even if your spouse thinks it's funny there is no place for it. That kind of behavior is negative and is one of Satan's disguised weapons to get you down. These are fiery darts that stick in there and fester and cause resentment. They build a foundation of hurt from which Satan can build a case against the hurtful spouse. He disguises it in the form of humor but he knows that no positive thing can result from it. Only hurt and resentment.

If you have always had that type of humor around you and have been programmed to use it everywhere you go, I have only one suggestion. Stop! This is a poison that must be eliminated from your soul. Start thinking of some positive things to joke and have fun with. If you look, there are plenty of good things to laugh about that won't tear someone down.

Use positive language when talking to your spouse. Talk to them as you would like to be talked to. It may be difficult for you to change your thought patterns and think more positive. To this, I only tell you that it will be worth every minute of the time you put into it. Eliminate the negative thoughts and think positive and your actions that follow will also become positive. Practice it daily until it becomes habit.

Practice thinking and talking positively with your spouse. Help each other as you go. Linda and I have a great tool to handle it when one of us says something negative. If I say something negative she will say to me in a loving tone of voice, "How could you say that differently?" or "How could you rephrase that?" We have prearranged ahead of time that when one of us asks that question that we will rephrase the question in a positive way. Here is an example: If I said, "Haven't you got dinner ready yet?" Linda would say to me, "How could you rephrase that?" Then I would think of how I could change that into a positive statement. I might say, "I am hungry dear, when will dinner be ready?" I could even say, "May I help you fix dinner?"

You can give this type of help to each other and it will help you change your negative attitude into a positive attitude. By being a help to your spouse and the spouse accepting the help, which is crucial, your relationship will improve dramatically and your love will grow even stronger. It is imperative that both of you are working on this together. Don't just see this as a *nagging* comment from one spouse to another. Use it in a loving way to truly help one another. By being positive toward each other all the time, the negative moments in your life will be much easier to recognize and handle. This tool alone will bring you so much happiness just by itself that you will be amazed.

When You Feel Down

What happens to you when you feel down and depressed? You may feel weary or beaten up by what is going on in your life. You may be tired of the same old thing. Discouraged by situations that you feel are out of your control. I am not talking about clinically diagnosed depression here. I am talking about just feeling down because of things that are happening around you. I think all of us have felt this from time to time. I know of people who seem to be the happiest people in the world when you are around them and yet when they are alone they can get very depressed.

As I said, all of us have experienced this at some point in our life and I am no different. This is something that again, your spouse can help you with. As a celestial couple, you need to be in tune with what your spouses needs are. When you see them feeling down and glum, that's the time for action. You see, feeling down and depressed though it seems natural for everyone to do, is one of Satan's weapons. You will be surprised to know that most of the time Satan is the one driving you to be depressed. Why do you think that is? God wants us to be happy. He says so.

> "Adam fell that men might be, and men are, that they might have joy." (*Book of Mormon*, 2 Nephi 2: 25)

One of God's purposes for man is that we gain joy by obedience to gospel law. As we are obeying the commandments we find joy. So who do you think doesn't want us to be happy? You are right. Satan would like nothing more than to drag us down from our happiness. He wants us to be as miserable as he is. Depression is one way to get us to lose our fight so that he has more influence over us. When you are depressed, do you feel like fighting? Do you just want to lie down and be by yourself? Do you just feel like it's no use in fighting back? Do you feel defeated? Look back at these questions. They are negative aren't they? These are things that Satan likes to see us feel. While we are feeling this way, he has a chance to get in there and whisper more negative self defeating statements that will further drag us down as we believe them.

Are you starting to see a pattern in how Satan works on us? He always starts with his whisperings trying to get you to believe that *you* are thinking these things. If you believe what he whispers, he will keep whispering to you with even more intensity. He leads us little by little down the spiral staircase to his dark and dreary dungeon.

How do you get out of this depression? The first thing is to recognize that you *are* depressed. This may be the most difficult stage. When you are depressed you don't feel like doing anything. You just want to be left alone. Of course, that's just when you need to do just the opposite. Once you recognize that you are depressed, get *How To Build Marriage Unity That Will Endure Throughout All Eternity* out and start reading. Find something that will help you. It may be reading the 3X5 scripture cards that you have pre written out. You may want to sing a church hymn. Pick out something that will help you get out of the mood you are in. I know what you are thinking, "What if I don't feel like singing a hymn?" Of course you won't feel like singing a hymn, you are depressed remember? I know this will be hard to do but do it anyway. The fact that you don't want to do one of these thing is proof enough that it is exactly what you need to do! You need to be successful in getting out of this depression.

Do you know what my definition of a successful person is? I believe a successful person does what he needs to do when it needs to be done while the unsuccessful person watches him. I want you to be successful! You have been given the tools in this book to improve your relationship with your eternal mate. So do what needs to be done right now. Take this book seriously and start working on what needs working on. Start today!

Let's see what other steps you will need to take to get out of this depression if you find it hard to do on your own. As I stated earlier, the first thing you need to do is recognize that you are depressed and do something about it. This is your first line of defense. But when you are not recognizing this then our second line of defense must take over. Let's see what should happen when your first line of defense is breached.

Many wars in history have been fought by setting up a first line of defense. This is the first barrier of men, guns, cannons or whatever was needed to fight the enemy on the front lines of battle. As the fight would rage on, if the enemy was too strong and the first line of defense was breached, the men would fall back to a position to where the next stronghold or line of defense was. This would be called the second line of defense.

This is how we are going to fight Satan with his onslaught of fiery darts. Your second line of defense is your spouse. You and your celestial partner need to be aware of each others moods. If you have been practicing saying positive comments to your mate and have been good at doing that and at some point you are looking down, not very talkative and are withdrawn, your spouse should recognize this. This is a time for your spouse to swing into action.

OK, let's say that you are the one that sees your spouse feeling down and depressed. What do you do? There are a number of things you can do. First of all, I am gong to tell you one thing you need to know. Your spouse is not going to like anything that you do or say to get them out of the depression. Why not? Because that is the nature of depression. They just want to be left alone. That's why you have got to proceed in a loving way. In no way can you be sarcastic or self righteous in the way you approach your spouse.

Let me tell you how my wife and I handle these situations. This may or may not apply to you depending upon how you as a couple normally handle everyday life. As for me and my wife, we always employ laughter every time we can. We believe that there has to be laughter in your life every day. Sometimes at the end of the day one of us will ask the other, "Have we laughed enough today?" If we have not, then we search for something to laugh about. If we cannot find something around us to laugh about, we may think back to a funny situation that happened to us last week and talk about it. We relive the comments of the situation that was so funny. We talk and laugh and make up new things to laugh about as we talk about the previous event. Laughter is the opposite of depression. It's hard to be depressed when you are laughing don't you think?

What I am getting at here is once you see that your spouse is a bit depressed, do something to make them laugh. Say something funny about your day or bring them back to another time when you were laughing together. Get excited and upbeat when you are trying to get them to laugh. Excitement and laughter is contagious. Your spouse will probably resist at first. Expect that and keep trying. I have even acted silly before in a way that my wife just had to laugh. The object is to get the depressed spouse to at least smile. A sincere smile would be ideal. Lead them along with a smile at first and eventually get them to laugh. You should know what would make your spouse laugh. This isn't the first time they have laughed right? So get into it.

Another way to help your spouse to get out of this gloom and doom attitude is to sing a hymn or happy song that you both like. Hold both hands and face each other as you sing. Look into each others eyes as you sing with smiles on your faces. You may even jump around and dance while you sing. Movement is very important to relieve the sluggishness of a depressed body. Sing it over and over again until the depression is lifted. I can see that a macho kind of man would not want to be seen dancing and singing with his wife like a couple of teenagers at a party. But, get over it. You are more important than your pride. If that's what it takes to get you out of the grips of Satan then that's what you need to do.

One more tool that can be taken out and used in this situation might be to kneel down and have a talk with your Heavenly Father. Ask Him to help you. You probably won't feel like praying but that is why you need to do it. The following quote is so true.

> "If you do not feel like praying, pray until you do feel like praying." ("Prayer," *True to the Faith,* (2004), 118–23)

If these methods don't work you might want to cast Satan out. It could be that you should consider getting a priesthood blessing or you may just want to use some of the other tools in *How To Build Marriage Unity That Will Endure Throughout All Eternity.* Do what is right and what works for you as a couple. Remember that a successful person does what he needs to do, when he needs to do it while the unsuccessful person watches him. I want you to be successful in getting out of your depression. Don't just sit on the sidelines watching the world go by. Get up and do something!

Yes, I know what you are thinking, "Can it really be that easy? How can you not be depressed when you have a lot on your mind? How can you not be depressed when you have certain responsibilities that have to be taken care of?" There are many more questions I am sure you have. If your depression is centered in something more serious that is happening in your life and can't be easily overcome, I suggest a heart to heart talk with your mate. Talk about the things that are troubling you. Get them off your chest so to speak. Let your mate help carry your load. Maybe a solution can be found between you. As I have talked with my eternal mate Linda, ideas and solutions have evolved from our discussion. Your mate may be able to help you see things from a different perspective. If your mate can't help you in what you are going through, at least they can have compassion for you and be supportive.

The bottom line is this. If you are depressed, you are not thinking straight. You are not on the top of your game. You are being pulled into a mindset of being defeated. A mindset of, *"it's not worth it,"* or *"there is nothing I can do about it,*" or whatever negative thoughts that Satan is whispering to you can leave you with a feeling of being defeated. He is pulling you off task. You cannot think clearly and positively while you are depressed. It is impossible and Satan knows this. That is why you must either bring yourself out of it or get help from your spouse. You must eliminate this treacherous self defeating behavior that keeps you under the influence of Satan.

Once you have arrived into the positive state of mind and are no longer depressed and feeling down, you must replace the empty space with something positive. At this point, you have used two of the three R's. You have *recognized* the depression, *removed* it and now you need to use the third R. You need to *replace* the empty hole with something positive. I suggest that you read some scriptures. You should write these out on some 3x5 cards so that they will be handy for you to get out when you need them. Here are a couple of the scriptures that we use to lift our spirits up.

> "Pray always, that you may come off conqueror, yeah that you may conquer Satan, and that you may escape the hand of the servants of Satan that do uphold his work." (*Doctrine and Covenants,* 10: 5)

> "Draw near unto me and I will draw near unto you; seek diligently and ye shall find me; ask, and ye shall receive, knock and it shall be opened unto you. Whatsoever ye shall ask the Father in my name, it shall be given unto you, that is expedient for you." (*Doctrine and Covenants,* 88: 63-64)

I have one last warning about depression. Satan would like nothing more than to get as many people as he can to *catch* this crippling disease. In other words, don't get sucked into this with your spouse. Some people who think they are showing compassion on the suffering spouse but by doing so will actually become depressed themselves. Don't get pulled in! Stand back and observe. What can you do to help them and boost up their spirits without being dragged into it yourself? I have already given you several examples above. Work this out between the two of you. See what works for you. Try different things and keep going. Don't give up on your spouse.

Remember, you are a great strength together, and together you will have happiness beyond measure if you will use these tools to fight off the master of evil.

POSITIVE BONDING

Right now, I want you to think about your spouse and see the good things about them. Get out a piece of paper right now and list all the things that you love about them. It could be the way they smile or the way they make you happy when they cook your dinner every night. You may like the way they stroke your face at night while you are in bed. It may be that you love the way they earn a living for the family. Maybe you appreciate that they are responsible. I want you to think of your own list of positive statements that you love about your spouse. You should come up with twenty or more statements. Don't just slough this off. I want you to think real hard about this. For some it may be easy to come up with twenty or more and for some it will be hard. Do it anyway. Stretch your mind and think positively. Don't put down a statement like, "Something I love about you is that you put up with my jokes." No no no. It has to be a positive statement like, "Something I love about you is that you laugh at my jokes." I can't stress enough of how these statements have to be said in a positive manner. Once you have completed this assignment you may read on.

Now, let's get to down to work here. I want you to put that list in front of you. OK, I want you to memorize each and every one of those statements. Yes, you heard me. Memorize them. It shouldn't be too hard because you thought of them and they are the things you love about your spouse. Now, the exercise goes like this. Once you have memorized these things, sometime this week I want you to sit down with your spouse where there will be no interruptions. Sit in a manner that you will be facing each other and that your faces are only about a foot apart. I want you to tell your spouse that you are going to tell them something and that they should not say anything until you are done. At which time, all you want them to say is, "Thank you."

With that said, I want you to look into your spouses eyes and say these words, "Something I love about you is," (then you will say one of the things you love about them that you memorized). Then you say again, "Something I love about you is," (then say another thing you love about them that you memorized). Continue down your memorized list until you are complete. Your statements should look like this:

- ☐ Something I love about you is that you are always happy.
- ☐ Something I love about you is that you keep yourself so healthy.
- ☐ Something I love about you is that you are so responsible.
- ☐ Something I love about you is that you are so beautiful.
- ☐ Something I love about you is the way you smile at me.
- ☐ Something I love about you is that you take such good care of the children.
- ☐ Something I love about you is that I can see your love for me in your actions.
- ☐ Something I love about you is that you are so thoughtful.
- ☐ Something I love about you is that you work so hard to make a living for our family.
- ☐ Something I love about you is that you always help me with chores around the house.
- ☐ Something I love about you is that I see you are 100 percent committed to our celestial marriage.

Ok, you get the point. Go on until you can't think of anything else. Then you can tell your spouse that you are done. They should say, "Thank you."

Until you do this, you have no idea what a positive bonding this will generate between you and your eternal mate. This is very powerful as you look into each others eyes and say these powerful affirmations and appreciations. You both will feel a tremendous boost in your feeling toward each other using this *something I love about you* tool. It is not necessary for the other spouse to repeat the exercise toward you at that same time, but it might be good on another day later that week. The moment is all about one spouse giving to the other and the other accepting the gift. It is not about who can top who's appreciation. This should not be competitive. It is about one giving their love to the other and appreciating them for who they are.

When you can see so many positives in a person and appreciate them for it, it will help you to see past their weaknesses and shortcomings a lot easier. This exercise should be repeated about every month or two for maximum bonding between you. It can be used in times of stress when one spouse needs the reassurance that they are worthwhile. Sometimes life can get overwhelming. We all need to know that we are good and that we matter in life. We all need to be appreciated and know that someone cares. This goes for our spouses. As time goes on we sometimes get caught up in so much day to day living that we just assume that our spouse knows how we feel about them. This is not true. We all need reinforcement. Make sure you keep this tool handy and use it regularly. This may be one of the best tools to keep you bonded together and keep your love alive so you can fight off the adversary.

In conclusion, it may seem like a lot of work to be positive in your thinking and your actions, and it will be at first. With anything, the more you work at it the easier it becomes. If what was presented in this chapter seems overwhelming just remember one thing, you don't have to do it all at once. Take it one step at a time. Start with one thing and when you are good at that start with another. Work with your spouse in setting up ahead of time how you will handle certain situations. I guarantee that as you concentrate on getting better at recognizing Satan's attacks, you *will* get better at it and it *will* get easier. Work on using the tools in this book once you recognize the demonic influences to remove them and then replace those negative thoughts with positive ones. Be positive and be on the Lord's side. Always be filling up your attitude bank with positive thoughts, statements and actions. Think positive thoughts about and say positive things to your spouse. Follow the three step program as outlined here if you see that your spouse is under Satan's influence. Recognize it and separate your spouse from Satan in your mind. Battle Satan not your spouse. Don't be offended or take anything personal. Work together with your spouse in all things to keep the demons from splitting you up. You are on the right road to success here. Both of you stay on the road and walk your way through life as the celestial couple. Make sure you implement the *something I love about you* tool so that you really bond together tightly. As the two of you exercise your faith in what you are doing and concentrate on making a positive difference in your lives, you will become a great strength together.

HELPFUL TOOLS IDENTIFIED OR EXPLAINED IN THIS CHAPTER:

1. Think positive.
2. Give thanks and be grateful to God for what you have.
3. You have free agency to choose.
4. Think positive about your spouse all the time.
5. Recognize Satan's influence in your mate and know that what they are saying is not of them.
6. Split what is happening into two different parts. Your mate's *real self* and Satan's influence upon your mate.
7. Choose *not to be offended* and stay calm.
8. Do not take it personally when you know your mate is under Satan's influence.
9. Cast out Satan.
10. Use the *stop stop stop* tool.
11. Accept help from your mate when they see Satan's influence is upon you.
12. Thank your mate for helping you.
13. Focus on the positive qualities of your mate and look past their imperfections.
14. Be grateful for all your eternal companion brings to your life.
15. Appreciate and build up your mate by making positive heart felt statements to them.
16. Avoid *cut downs* of any kind to your spouse.
17. *How could you say that differently* tool used in a loving manner.
18. Prearrange ahead of time how you will handle certain situations like the *how could you say that differently* tool.
19. Laughter.
20. Recognize you are depressed.
21. 3X5 scripture cards.
22. Sing a church hymn.

23. Use the second line of defense, your spouse to help you.
24. Dance while you sing together.
25. Prayer.
26. Talk with your mate to help you find a solution.
27. Priesthood blessing.
28. Have compassion and be supportive of your mate.
29. Use the three R's tool; recognize, remove and replace.
30. *What I love about you* tool.

5
ME, CHANGE?

This is a great question. Do I have to change? People are in a constant state of change. Sometimes these could be major changes and sometimes little changes or both. Change could be one of the hardest things for people to do. We are creatures of habit, right? Yes we are. We start doing something a certain way and may have done it for years and suddenly someone wants us to do it some other way. How dare them!

Me, change? I am the way I am and that's it. Why should I have to change? Why don't you change? We think of all kinds of excuses so we don't have to change, don't we? Change is real hard for most people, especially major changes like moving from one state to another. It has been said that change is the only thing that is constant. What does that mean? It means that everything is always changing around us. If we don't change with it, we will be left in the dust.

The change I am going to talk about is the change within our relationship with our eternal mate. If you don't think anything changes in your relationship with your spouse, then you haven't been married more than five minutes! There are many changes occurring that have to be addressed and accounted for. As these changes occur, adjustments have to be made to the way you think, act and what you say or do not say. In life, you are constantly learning new things as you go. There is no life manual to tell you step by step what to do, think or say. You have to *fly by the seat of your pants* so to speak.

Anyone who has had children knows that it would be much easier if each child came with an instruction manual on how to raise them based on their individual personality. There are many books written on how to raise children but none that will be specific to each individual child. Therefore, you are left to raise them as best you can as you discover how to raise them one step at a time. Each time you try something and it doesn't work, you change your approach and try something else.

This approach is how your entire life is governed, is it not? You may study a situation, look at ways to approach it, investigate and come up with your best answer or way to execute a plan. You complete the task based on your knowledge and it either works out or it doesn't. If it doesn't work out, you rethink the plan and come up with something else. You simply change what you did the first time and hope for the best.

CHANGE CREATES UNITY

This is a great quote from my wife Linda. "People hate to change, but if they want their relationship to change for the better, they better do something about it. They better change themselves." Working on changing yourself and not your mate is the key to having a better relationship. You just can't keep pointing the finger at your mate, even though it seems so *natural* to do so. It is always easier to point the finger at someone else rather than look at what you are doing. This is because most people do not like to change. They want other people to change for them. They want to be right. They don't want to take the blame. "Point the finger and get the blame away from me," they think. "You are the one that is wrong and you should change your ways," is what they say. If the other person does not want to change and they think that they are the ones that are right, nothing will change. There will always be conflict and disunity.

The idea is to become *one* with your eternal mate even as Christ is one with Heavenly Father. How can you become one when no one will change so that there will be harmony within your home? When we point the finger at our mate, we are attacking ourselves. Since we are becoming *one* with each other, an attack made on your mate would be an attack on yourself.

You know what the definition of insanity is, don't you? Insanity is when you do the same thing over and over again expecting a different result. Are you becoming insane when it comes to improving your relationship with your eternal companion? Are you doing the same thing you have always done expecting your mate to change so that things will get better? This has got to stop! Look at what you are doing. Take responsibility for your actions. Why are you so stubborn? Shake it loose. Look at the overall big picture.

CHANGE THE WAY YOU THINK

Many couples get upset over small things, many small things. They get upset over the toilet seat being left up, or the toothpaste being left out on the counter, or the light in the bedroom being left on, or "You are late again," or "You were home all day, why is the house a mess?" Are these annoyances of any eternal importance? I am sure you can think of many more such menial situations that really don't make a hill of beans when you take the eternities into consideration. I am not saying that any of these things are unimportant. I am saying that they are not important enough to fight or argue over. Now that's a different subject I will discuss in a different chapter. For now, let's get back to change.

What can we change about these situations? What is important about these situations and what is not? What can we change to make the situations better? What can you change within yourself that will make you happier and feel more happiness towards your mate?

Let's look at an example. The usual complaint among many women is that the man leaves the toilet lid up after going to the bathroom. The most common comments I have heard from women is that it looks better for the seat to be down and she doesn't want to sit down and fall in because the seat is up. From most men's point of view, he doesn't care what it looks like and feels that it is just as easy for her to put it down as it is for him to put it up. Both sides seem right don't they? Well, I am not here to settle this argument once and for all. That is not my purpose. My purpose is to see what is needed for change.

Both of you need to be aware of each others feelings on the subject. Yes, you must come to an agreement as to what the desired action should be, or do you? Each of you have in your mind what you want this action to be, right? Each of you want the other person to change their way of doing things, or at least allow you to do what you want. What is the answer? To answer that, you need to ask the right questions. What are the right questions? The correct questions are: What does this toilet seat have to do with my eternal progression? How will my eternal marriage be affected if the toilet seat is up or down? Does it really matter?

You must change your way of thinking right now. Husbands, your thinking should be this way. Would putting the toilet seat down make your wife happy and cause harmony in your relationship? If the answer is no, then don't worry. If the answer is yes, then by all means put it down. If this makes your wife happy, then do this no matter what logic or rationalization you assign to it. Some decisions have to be based on practicality or emotional thought while throwing logic out the window. Wives, you should think like this. When he leaves the toilet seat up, if I nag him about it, would this be worth the negative feelings it will cause between us as a celestial couple? Is it worth my husband's happiness as well as my own to let it go? If you get upset about it and yell at your husband, will that make things better or worse? I think you know the answer.

Certainly not all decisions can be made as simply as this, but if you look at the decisions you make when keeping in mind your eternal purpose, you will find less and less to argue and be upset about your mate. The change is within you. You need to change the way you think about your life. You need to change the way you think about your mate. You need to change the way you think from negative to positive thinking.

Change can be hard and it can be easy. It is all based on how you think about it. A lifelong habit will not be easy to correct. It will be especially hard if you carry negative thoughts about it while you are trying to change. Don't think stuff like, "I am just doing this for her.

Why do I have to change? I hate doing this. He is the winner because now I am doing what he says." These are all self defeating thoughts. When you are making changes, do a thorough job of it. Start thinking, "This change is going to improve my relationship with my mate. What I am doing now will make them happy and in return, it will make me happy. I enjoy pleasing my eternal companion." This positive self talk will help you keep that positive attitude and reinforce the changes that you are making until they become habit. This will indeed enhance your relationship with your spouse.

What about big changes in one's life? Let's say that you lived in Idaho where all of your family resides. You are used to being around your parents, siblings and their children. Suddenly, he gets a job offer in Arizona that simply can't be passed up. This is a big change, especially for women. Most women are so family oriented that they would feel lost without their family around. A move like this would usually be hard for the wife. Sometimes it would be hard for the husband, but usually men go with the flow. A man's got to do what a man's got to do, right?

So the couple moves to Arizona. Put yourself in the place of this couple and picture this. You are away from your family, it's hot there, you have no friends, you don't know what the schools are like, you don't know where any of the stores are, etc. There are a lot of negatives right? Well, you still use the same approach. Do not think these negative thoughts. Start thinking positive thoughts no matter how hard it is. Think, "We have a new opportunity here. This is a chance for the husband to advance in his career and we'll be making more money to support the family better. I get to see a different part of the country and have new experiences. I get to meet new people and make new friends. I am here for a reason. What positive contribution can I make while I am here?" These are thoughts that you should have and more.

Look at what life brings you and don't look back to what might have been. Looking back and wondering or worrying about what you might have had if you had stayed will only bring you heartache. You will never be happy where you are until you let go of the past. Look toward your future and what it will become.

Remember Laman and Lemuel from the *Book of Mormon?* They complained all the way out of Jerusalem and all the way to the promise land. They were never satisfied. They always kept looking back to Jerusalem and wanting to go back. Had they gone back, they would have been destroyed along with that great city or been carried away captive to some far away place. How happy would they have been then? They never looked at the new promise land as an opportunity to enhance their lives or make it better. Right up to the end they were cursing their brother Nephi for their afflictions.

Let us not curse our eternal companions for any seemingly terrible afflictions. A move out of an environment you were comfortable with into a *foreign land* could prove to be a blessing in disguise. Be grateful for everything that comes your way, including challenges where changes are needed.

Nag Nag Nag

Wow, isn't that a powerful heading? Well, I really have only one word to say about nagging. The word is, don't. I could probably stop there and you would get my drift. Alas, I do have to say more. No one that I know likes someone else to nag at them. Nagging is where one spouse constantly tells the other the same thing over and over again, hoping to change that spouse's behavior. The spouse on the receiving end only gets more irritated and for the most part, rebels against the nagging spouse. Nagging doesn't do anyone any good. Both spouses are irritated and nothing good is accomplished.

Another thing that goes along with nagging is nitpicking your spouse. Don't watch every move they make so you can pick at them. Don't pick apart every word they say. Don't try to find fault and pick at everything they do. If you do this, you are not helping them, you are pulling them down. Both nagging and nitpicking are two of Satan's powerful tools to cause dissention and disharmony between couples. Don't let Satan's influence get to you.

What do you think needs to be done instead of nagging and nitpicking? Of course you know what is needed by now, don't you? Better communication would be a start. Recognizing that this is a negative behavior would be another, right? Remembering that you are both 100 percent committed to your relationship would be nice right now.

How about being quick to forgive? How about loving unconditionally? What about not being offended? Be the master of your emotions. Use some of the tools to get rid of Satan and his whisperings. Recognize this weakness in yourself and work on overcoming it. You see, there are lots of things covered in this book that you could focus your attention on rather than nagging, right? I knew you would see it that way.

Why Am I Beating Myself Up Over This?

Change for the better is hard for a lot of people. As you read through this book, some of the concepts and ideas may seem to be more than you can do right now. To this I say, "Congratulations!" No one after reading this book or any other will become perfect at what they read right away. As with anything, you need to take the first step and then another. Walk toward your goal one step at a time. I know that you know you have a ways to go in accomplishing what has been written here. It will be just like the age old question, "How do you eat an elephant?" "One bite at a time," is the answer.

Here's what is going to happen to you as you read and try to put into practice these principles. First, you are going to say to yourself, "This is what I need to do to help myself. I know I need to change what I am doing to have a better life. I know I need to change my thinking and my actions in order to attain the celestial kingdom." Then, Satan is going to do his best to discourage you from accomplishing your desire. He is going to suggest that this is an impossible goal you have set out to achieve. He will suggest to you that no one can accomplish what is written here. Satan knows your weaknesses and will play off of them to discourage you. He knows where to throw those fiery darts. He knows how to make you feel bad when you feel you *can't* accomplish what you have set out to do.

Satan tries to make you feel bad by whispering things like, "*You know you should do what the book says, but you can't seem to do it. You are worthless. You should feel terrible because you are not living the way you should. You don't deserve this help anyway because you can't live up to it. Why are you even trying, you know you can't do it? Who do you think you are anyway, some saintly person?*" Satan is whispering things into your mind to persuade you to beat yourself up over not being able to be perfect right away! Don't let him do that!

Look, when you learned to drive a car, were you perfect at it just as soon as you got behind the wheel? I don't know about you but I was instructed in a driver's education class in high school for a year before I even got behind the wheel. The teacher instructed us about the mechanics of the automobile as well as the rules of the road. In addition to that, I had watched my parents drive for years. I knew every move they made. So, I had all that knowledge behind me when I sat behind the wheel for the first time to drive. I knew all the mechanics about how to drive a vehicle with a manual transmission which had a clutch and a three speed shift on the column. I knew how to steer the vehicle I was sitting in. I knew I had to stop when the light was red and go when it was green. I knew all that stuff but when I turned on the key and went to let out the clutch to get going, what do you think happened? Yeah, you guessed it. I popped the clutch and the vehicle lunged forward and died. I killed it! Oh how embarrassed I was. I had seen my parents do this time and time again flawlessly. I tried again and again until I gave it the right amount of gas as I let the clutch out. Once I got the vehicle moving, the next step was to steer it in the right direction while looking for traffic and obstacles so I didn't run into anything. Oh no, now I needed to shift into second gear while using the clutch thing again. Whoops! I forgot to let off the gas and the engine revved up and when I let the clutch out we jerked forward again. This wasn't going well. Before I could shift into third, my dad told me to pull over and stop. As I did so, I forgot to push in the clutch and the vehicle did some more jerking and the engine died again.

With this first experience of driving, I could have just been too embarrassed to ever try to drive again. I could have just said, "Forget it, it's too hard!" I could have let it get to me and just quit. I didn't. By listening to my father's instruction and working at it, I became better and better at working the clutch and gas pedal together to create the perfect harmony between the two so that I had smooth starts and stops. I became as proficient as my instructor.

Now, let's put you in the driver's seat for a minute. I am not talking about being behind the wheel of a car though. I am talking about learning one of the concepts taught here. Think of it like you were driving a car with a manual transmission and popping the clutch. You *must not listen* to Satan and his evil whisperings. You must change the way you are thinking so you will recognize his whisperings. Don't beat yourself up if at first you don't succeed at what you are trying to accomplish. Changing for the better is not easy but you must continue working at it. No matter what negative thing happens to you, use the tools in this book to help you to overcome that situation in a positive manner. Keep practicing so you can get real good at it. Don't give up. Change will get easier as you go along.

If you don't succeed at first, stop and look at what you have learned. What happened and how did you react? Analyze how you could have reacted differently. What could you do to improve if that situation should arise again? Apply what you have learned to the next situation. Just like I learned to drive a manual transmission vehicle, I practiced until I got it right. I saw what I was doing wrong and corrected it. I worked on one thing at a time.

OK, let's get back to Satan's whisperings. Now that you know this will take practice and you are not expected to be perfect right away, dispel those demonic whisperings. Don't give them any thought or emotion. Yeah, I can hear you now. You are saying, "How can I not give it emotion?" Yes, this will be hard at first, just like driving a manual transmission car. It all comes back to recognizing those satanic whispering in the first place. You must change the way you think. This is not of you! Think about that. This is not of you. Recognize that the negative thoughts are from Satan. Self defeating thoughts are the whisperings of the devil! He wants you to feel defeated by whispering things to doubt yourself, to feel like you can't measure up, like you shouldn't even try, like you are not worth bettering yourself and by not allowing yourself to see that you are more powerful than him. You can overcome these whisperings and self defeating thoughts that come into your mind. *Do not let Satan influence you!* You are more powerful than him.

As you read through this book you must change the way you think as you discover all kinds of ways to get Satan out of your life. Use them over and over again. This is an ongoing battle with him. You must take control and cast Satan out or read scriptures, or pray for help, or sing a church hymn or whatever tool works for you to get him out of your mind and stop his whisperings. Then fill your mind with positive encouraging thoughts that will help you towards your goal. Change your thought process by thinking positive thoughts like, "I know I can overcome my anger, I am a positive person, I will not take it personally what negative things people say to me, I will not become offended, I am a child of God and will act accordingly, and so on.

Pray to your Heavenly Father for help to make these positive changes. If you pray with a sincere heart that you want to be able to not take negative things so personally, He will help you. If you want help with any of your weaknesses you must ask in faith and He will help you. Ask Him to help you overcome your weaknesses and help you turn them into strengths. Ask Him to help you have a change of heart. I know from personal experience that He is there for each of us. If you want to change for the better, He will help and guide you and through the Holy Ghost He will prompt you to do better. The only way you can effect permanent positive change in your life is if you overcome Satan's temptings and whisperings. Each time you overcome these temptations you will become stronger and stronger.

In conclusion, be glad for the changes in your life. Embrace change. Learn to love it. Without it, we are stuck in a rut and cannot progress. If you don't believe it, let me ask you one question. Are you perfect? There was only one person ever to walk the earth that can say yes to that question, and that is our Savior. Other than Him, we all have to make changes in order to reach the celestial kingdom.

It is time for change and change is good. Make changes as needed and do it with a cheerful heart looking in the right direction. The right direction you should be looking in is how can I perfect myself in the eyes of my eternal mate so that there is no contention in our household? Don't sweat the small stuff. What is most important to our relationship and what changes can I make to improve it? What is important and what can I let go? Discuss these changes with your mate so you can both be working on the same page.

Nagging or nitpicking does not help your mate. It does not change behavior. It only causes dissention. Use other tools in this book to help each other change that behavior.

Do not beat yourself up if you cannot make immediate changes and be perfect right away. Work on what you can work on. If it seams overwhelming, just work on one thing at a time until you get good at it. Then work on something else. Don't get discouraged. Don't let Satan get to you as he whispers negative things into your mind. Recognize his whisperings and get him out of your thinking process. Eliminate him with the tools within these pages and replace those negative thoughts with good positive ones. If you don't succeed at first, look at how you handled the situation and analyze it. See what you did and how you can improve upon it next time. If you are truly trying to get good at applying the principles in this book, you will succeed at accomplishing your goal. You cannot fail! You are simply taking one step at a time toward perfection.

Seek for the guidance of your Heavenly Father to guide you and help you along the way. If you have the faith that you can overcome your weaknesses, you will overcome them and be much happier. Continue to work with your eternal mate. As you work together in making changes and as you learn to drive the same vehicle at the same time toward the same goal (celestial kingdom), you can't help but become a great strength together.

HELPFUL TOOLS IDENTIFIED OR EXPLAINED IN THIS CHAPTER:

1. Work on changing yourself.
2. Be aware of each others feelings on various subjects.
3. Ask yourself these questions: How will my eternal marriage be affected by this difference of opinion I have with my mate? Will it matter in the eternities? If not, I will let it go.
4. Think positive statements about the changes you are making and how it will improve your relationship with your spouse.
5. Avoid looking back at what might have been. Look forward with a cheerful heart to a new and bright future.
6. As you make positive changes and are not perfect about them right away, don't beat yourself up about it. Just keep working on them until you are successful.
7. Recognize Satan's whisperings.
8. Do not give Satan's whisperings any thought or emotion.

9. Cast Satan out.
10. Read scriptures.
11. Pray.
12. Sing a church hymn.
13. Fill your mind with positive thoughts.
14. Do not take negative things said to you in a personal way.
15. Do not become offended.

6

How Can I Forgive
After What They Did?

All of us have at one time or another been challenged by another individual. By this I mean someone has offended us, made us angry by what they said or did, or acted against one of our loved ones in such a way that hurt us. There are as many ways that this can happen as there are grains of sand on the seashore. Each of us is different and can be hurt in a variety of ways. We can be hurt physically, mentally, emotionally and spiritually.

I don't think it is necessary to describe all the ways we can be hurt physically, mentally, emotionally or spiritually because most of us have had that unfortunate experience. How did you feel when those hurts were afflicted upon you? What emotions did it stir up in your mind when the person *did* that to you? Did you want to get them back? Did it rage in your mind for several days, weeks, months or years? How did it affect the rest of your life? Did you have trouble sleeping during the time you held this rage in your heart? Were you tough to live with while you were holding that grudge? How do you think it affects your job or dealings with your kids and mate? These are just some of the questions you should ask yourself when you have not forgiven someone for offending or hurting you.

Have you ever felt that when someone offended you that they should come to you and ask for your forgiveness before you forgave them? Have you felt that unless they came groveling at your feet there would be no way that you would forgive them? In my research I have not found in any book including the scriptures where it says that they have to ask your forgiveness for you to be able to forgive them. In fact, no where does it say that they even have to deserve to be forgiven for you to forgive them. Here is what the scriptures say:

> "I, the Lord, will forgive whom I will forgive, but of you it is required to forgive all men." (*Doctrine and Covenants,* 64: 10)

This scripture does not say, forgive all men, if they confess to you or ask for your forgiveness. There is no requirement attached to this. You are *required* to forgive all men. Why should we be required to do this? The passage just before this one gives you a good enough reason.

> "Wherefore, I say unto you, that ye ought to forgive one another; for he that <u>forgiveth</u> not his brother his trespasses standeth condemned before the Lord; for there remaineth in him the greater sin." (*Doctrine and Covenants,* 64: 9)

Wow, is this not reason enough? If you don't forgive your brother, you stand condemned before the Lord because you have committed a greater sin than the person who offended you. I don't know about you but I don't want to be condemned before the Lord because of someone else. Keep this in mind as I discuss this further.

Well, this is not the only reason that we should forgive. Have you ever had something happen to you and you kept thinking about it throughout the day. As you thought about what that other person said and what he did, your emotions get stirred up and you feel upset. Your muscles get tight in your neck and your stomach tightens up. You feel a lump in your throat as you are consumed with anger. Then you start thinking of what you said and what you should have said and how you can get back at them. All these negative thoughts drag you down and cause you to be stressed out. Who do you think you are hurting? Are you hurting the person that you are thinking about? I don't think so. More than likely they are not even aware that you are thinking these negative thoughts about them. They might even be clueless that they even did something to offend you. So, by your thinking about this person and having all these negative thoughts in your mind, you are only hurting you, right?

It only stands to reason one thing. If they are not even aware that they did anything wrong, they are not going to apologize and ask for your forgiveness are they? If they are not aware that you are even thinking about them, you are not getting back at them are you? It doesn't matter whether they deserve forgiveness or not, we are required to forgive all men. If the only person that is hurting over what they did or said is you, then why not forgive them? Doesn't that make sense? Of course it does.

You are the only one in control of you! You have the power to control how you feel about the situation. You can choose to feel angry and resentful about a person or you can choose to forgive and let it go. It's your choice.

ILLNESS CAUSED BY LACK OF FORGIVENESS

Did you know that it is becoming better known that how and what we think can cause certain illnesses? As we think negatively and get stressed out, this can cause different parts of our body to become ill. I believe that many of the illnesses today are directly caused by people's negative thinking.

Remember the movie I told you about in chapter 4. It was *What in the Bleep Do We Know.* The scientist found out that water could be changed on a molecular level by just taping pieces of paper to the container of water with negative words written on them. Just think how you are affected by your negative thoughts since you are made up of over 50 percent water! Negative thoughts and actions are certainly more powerful than writing on pieces of paper. Lack of forgiveness is definitely thinking negatively.

Don't get sick over the lack of forgiveness. By not forgiving someone you can actually cause your body to get sick. Not only that, but your sickness can spread to your eternal mate. If you carry this grudge around with you, it will manifest itself in other areas in your life. It will affect your communication and feelings toward your eternal companion. I can hear you thinking, "How can it affect my mate when the anger I feel is not directed at them?" I will tell you how. It is all about how you feel inside. If you are angry and hurt about something someone did or said it will stir up those negative emotions in your body. This will affect your total overall emotional state of mind. You will be in a negative mode when you come into contact with anyone, even your mate.

If you don't believe this, try this little experiment. I want you to get angry with a happy smile on your face or try to laugh while you are angry. It is impossible to do both at the same time. Your emotions whether negative or positive will be one or the other. If you are so stirred up with negative emotions from the grudge you are holding, you will be negative towards your mate. Things that you say and do will be governed by the negativity. You might complain more or get more agitated at small irritations that would not have bothered you in the past. Things that have irritated you just a little before are now huge irritations that may cause you to *blow up*. You tend to attract more negative things into your life to be angry about. This is a pattern you must break. How do you break this pattern? Forgiveness is what we have been talking about.

You say, "OK, I get it. But they keep offending me. How can I forgive them when they keep doing it?" Well, let's go to the authority on forgiveness for the answer to that question.

> "Then came Peter to Him, and said, Lord, how oft shall my brother sin against me, and I forgive him? till seven times? Jesus saith unto him, I say not unto thee, until seven times: but, until <u>seventy</u> times seven." (*Bible*, King James Version, Matthew 18: 21 & 22)

Sounds to me what Jesus is saying is to forgive them no matter how many times they trespass against you. If the shoe was on the other foot, wouldn't you like to be forgiven as many times as you could? Here is one last reason that you should forgive someone who has trespassed against you. The Lord will forgive those who forgive others.

> "For if ye forgive men their trespasses, your heavenly Father will also forgive you: But if ye forgive not men their trespasses, neither will your Father forgive your trespasses." (*Bible*, King James version, Matthew 6: 14 &15)

So, we are required by the Lord to forgive and then he blesses us by forgiving us as we forgive others. Not only that but we will find peace from within us by forgiving and letting it go. The letting go is essential to the forgiving process. Once you have forgiven someone, you must let it go and think no more about it. Let it fade through the healer of time. Clear your mind of the emotion attached to it. You will still remember what the offense was as a distant memory but treat the person as though it never happened. This may be difficult but it is possible.

We have learned about why we should forgive. Now let's see how we should ask for forgiveness. This may be one of the hardest things that you can do, to ask someone for forgiveness. It may not be easy because it strips away your pride. Not many people like to admit that they were wrong. It is a humbling experience to truly admit to someone that you were wrong and to ask for forgiveness. This is a character building experience and is necessary for you to become a celestial couple. Going to someone, especially your eternal mate, and asking them for forgiveness is crucial to a successful eternal marriage. Pay close attention to the following section.

WHEN WE FORGIVE EACH OTHER

When the time comes that we have done something that we shouldn't have and we upset our spouse, we need to ask forgiveness. There are a couple ways that we can do this. We can do it the lame way or the right way. Ok, I said the lame way. To me it's lame because there is no participation on the other person's part. This is where you say, "Sorry." I say this is lame because there are several ways in which you can say it. You have heard someone say, "Sorry." as they are walking out the door. They may say it as they shrug their shoulders, like whoops, "Sorry." You know what I mean. The way they say it really has no impact or meaning behind it. Sometimes if the person that is being apologized to is so mad that when the offender says, "Sorry." he says, "Well, you should be!" There just isn't the sincerity behind it.

On the other hand, if someone asks, "Forgive me," or "Please forgive me," it takes on a new meaning. The person asking is expecting a response. Sometimes the one being asked to forgive the other will say something like, "Oh don't worry about it." or "You are forgiven." or something nice like that. Or they might still want to talk about it until it is clear in their head that they will forgive you. Either way, this is the best method for asking.

Now, as for the forgiveness part of it, I feel it is important for you to say the words, "I forgive you." It puts finality into your forgiveness. It doesn't leave it open for wonderment like, "Don't worry about it." That can be taken a couple different ways. If I said that to you it could mean that I have no problem with it right at the moment but that I am really still not over what you are apologizing for and I haven't fully forgiven you. It could mean that I have forgiven you totally. It could mean that I haven't forgiven you at all and I just don't want to talk or think about it right now. Do you see what I mean? Wouldn't you want to make sure someone understood your meaning, especially when you are forgiving someone? If you don't give that finality and assurance that you have forgiven them then how do you think they would feel? As in the case of, *Don't worry about it*, the person being forgiven can think one of three or more ways. This can cause them to feel for example that you haven't forgiven them and feel sorrowful, even though you have totally forgiven them. The whole point of forgiveness is to start the healing process. If the forgiven one doesn't know he is forgiven for sure, how can he begin healing? I don't like to be held in limbo like that. Yes, you can go on with life but you are still wondering if that other person is still holding a grudge.

So, I have found the best way to forgive your spouse is to say, "I forgive you." Now this may not be possible for you at the time that forgiveness is asked for. You may not be able to forgive the person at that moment. If you are new at this and haven't quite mustered up the forgiveness in your heart, you may need some time to work through it in your mind. I suggest praying about it and asking Heavenly Father to help you. His way is best.

Pray that your heart will be filled with compassion for your spouse. Pray for the unconditional love you need to see past their words or deeds so that you can love the person inside. Pray for help to not be judgmental. Ask for help that you may not take it personally as to what was said or done. Ask for Heavenly Father to help you to forgive and let it go. These are some of the steps I have found needed to get from a strong, *hating* that person to the understanding that I love the person and forgiving the action he or she did. Don't just say you forgive a person just because you think you should say it. You need to truly feel that you forgive them, tell them you forgive them and then let it go. Think no more about it and especially don't bring it up again if the same situation repeats itself. Truly let it go. Let each situation stand by itself. If you don't, you truly haven't let it go the first time.

Once you have prayed and felt the forgiveness a couple times concerning your spouse, you will find it easier to forgive when things happen. As you grow closer together and see that each of you is working on the things that have been challenges in the past, it will be easier to forgive your spouse. We are human and can be easily tricked by Satan to fall into old habits. Satan would like nothing more than for us to hold grudges against one another. Set yourself free from these grudges and resentments by forgiving and seeking earnest forgiveness.

Linda and I have taken this one step further. After the moment of forgiveness has taken place we face each other, clasp our hands together as our hands and arms hang down. We look into each others eyes and smile as we sing our *victory song*. It is actually the chorus from the hymn "Behold! A Royal Army," (*Hymns*, N. 251)

> Victory, victory, through Him that redeemed us,
> Victory, victory thru Jesus Christ our Lord,
> Victory victory victory,
> Thru Jesus Christ our Lord.

As we sing the last two lines, we raise our clasped hands high in the air with big smiles as we sing looking into each others eyes. It is an awesome moment as we are victorious and we feel cleansed. Cleansed from the negative feelings from whatever happened previously. Our spirits connect and we feel healed spiritually, mentally and emotionally. It's like a renewing of our love for each other. A fantastic experience if you haven't tried it. Even you macho guys can do it. Come on, enjoy the moment would you?

This is the pattern in which Linda and I have decided to pull together and be a great strength together. Anything you can do to strengthen your bond with your spouse is imperative! Satan's fiery darts can strike at any moment and you need to be prepared for the fiery storm. Sometimes the storm is a little one and it's easy to get through. Sometimes it's a hurricane and look out. If you are not bonded tightly together without wedges between you, it might be like riding a bucking bronco with nothing to hold onto. You need that bonding with your spouse to be safe and secure so that nothing will separate you.

I am not saying that you need to do as Linda and I have done in singing the *victory song*. I am saying that you must choose what's right for you. The both of you should decide what it is that will bring you together after you have had your *moments*. It's OK if it is a little silly at first. Just do something that will create that bonding right after you have had something happen and then you have resolved it. I am not just talking about making love here. That can be done as well. I am talking about something you can do when other people are around or when you are out somewhere. Of course we don't sing our victory song in front of people. We go off to a secluded place or go to the car and sing it, Ok, you get the point. There is no sense in beating a dead horse right?

Suffice it to say, always ask for someone to forgive you. Always say I forgive you and have a little victory song or dance or whatever you need to create that unity once again. As you do this and quickly forgive each other by having unconditional love in your hearts, you will find that the two of you will have yet another tool in place that will bond you together for an eternity.

So, what have we learned in this chapter? The Lord requires us to forgive one another and if we don't, there remains the greater sin in him that does not forgive. The Lord knows what being unforgiving will do to us. It will cause us all kinds of grief mentally, emotionally, physically and spiritually. We should forgive one another as many times as necessary even if someone trespasses against us many times the same way. Not only must we forgive, but we should ask for forgiveness. Don't just say, "Sorry." Make sure you are asking forgiveness in the right way with the right attitude. As you forgive and ask for forgiveness, you will see an attitude change within yourself and you will find it easier to forgive others. This will bring peace to your soul. When you have forgiven your spouse or have been forgiven by your mate, join together in a *victory* celebration. This will create a bonding between you and your eternal mate as you recognize that you had a victory over Satan. By quickly forgiving, this will help you achieve unconditional love for your mate. By forgiving yourself and those around you quickly, you will be forgiven by your Heavenly Father. Keep these things in mind as you and your mate work together toward perfection. If you practice this on a daily basis your spirits will become as one as you become a great strength together.

HELPFUL TOOLS IDENTIFIED OR EXPLAINED IN THIS CHAPTER:

1. Forgive one another even if they don't ask for forgiveness.
2. After forgiving, let it go and think no more about it.
3. Clear your mind of the emotion attached to what you have just forgiven.
4. Treat the person you forgave as though it never happened.
5. Ask forgiveness in the right way. Say, "Please forgive me."
6. When forgiving someone say, "I forgive you."
7. Pray for compassion and unconditional love towards your mate.
8. Do not judge your mate.
9. Do not take what was said personally.
10. Love the person and forgive the action they did.
11. Tell them you forgive them.
12. Sing a *victory* song together.
13. Forgive yourself.

7

ME, OFFENDED?

What does offended mean anyway? One dictionary defines offend as: to cause displeasure, anger, resentment, or wounded feelings. To be displeased or disagreeable. To be offended would then mean that someone or something caused you displeasure, anger, resentment, wounded feelings, or caused you to be displeased or disagreeable. So, this doesn't sound too positive. To be offended is a rather negative response, don't you think? Here we go again, that positive and negative thing again. It's easy to spot now, right? Good, now let's move on. Here is part of a talk given by Elder David A. Bednar on the subject of not being offended.

> "When we believe or say we have been offended, we usually mean we feel insulted, mistreated, snubbed, or disrespected. And certainly clumsy, embarrassing, unprincipled, and mean-spirited things do occur in our interactions with other people that would allow us to take offense. However, it ultimately is impossible for another person to offend you or to offend me. Indeed, believing that another person offended us is fundamentally false. To be offended is a *choice* we

make; it is not a *condition* inflicted or imposed upon us by someone or something else. In the grand division of all of God's creations, there are things to act and things to be acted upon (*Book of Mormon*, 2 Nephi 2:13–14). As sons and daughters of our Heavenly Father, we have been blessed with the gift of moral agency, the capacity for independent action and choice. Endowed with agency, you and I are agents, and we primarily are to act and not just be acted upon. To believe that someone or something can *make* us feel offended, angry, hurt, or bitter diminishes our moral agency and transforms us into objects to be acted upon. As agents, however, you and I have the power to act and to choose how we will respond to an offensive or hurtful situation." (General Conference, October 2006, Elder David A. Bednar, *italics added*)

Now that we know it is a choice, we should choose not to be offended. When you just begin to feel displeased or irritated at someone you should stop yourself before it goes any further. Do not attach any emotion to it. It's your choice, right? If your irritation escalates and your emotion starts welling up within you, it will take you to the next level of feeling offended. So don't step on that escalator! That's one ride you don't need to go on. Stop! You need to get out of the negative mode. The negative mode is where Satan has hold of you. You are on his side of the football field where he has more influence over you. The closer to the goal line on his side of the field he can get you, the more influence he has over you. If you think of it in those terms, you'll see where his *goal* is. His goal is to make you as miserable as he is and to drag you down to hell with him. The more negative of a mode he can get you into the more he can influence you to do what he wants. Satan is the father of contention and lies. He would like nothing more than to keep you in the negative mode as long as he can so that he can stir up contention and arguments. His half truths make you feel justified in your negative comments. So, snap out of it!

FOCUS ON THE POSITIVE

Look and listen for something positive to focus on. As you are thinking of something negative because of the irritation, you need to shock your brain by thinking something positive. Have fun with it. Satan hates laughter and fun. He is into negative depressing lonely self defeating attitudes. So have fun with it. If something irritates you, think of something funny or amusing to play off the irritating thing.

Here is an example: John is sitting there quietly with his wife Sally. Well, Sally has this nervous habit of putting her thumbs together and rubbing her thumbnails together back and forth making a "clicking" noise about every two seconds. Not only that but each time she makes the clicking sound the arm that is pressed up against John suddenly jerks at every click. This irritates John because he feels this jerking motion and hears the clicking and he wants to sit still and hear silence (How anyone hears silence I'll never know). So, what is John to do?

He has told her time and time again that this irritates him. She is obviously not going to change her habit. So, John decides to make it a fun thing. He looks at Sally's thumbs and as she is clicking them and imagines popcorn flying out with every click. Popcorn flying here and there and he is trying to catch it with his tongue. One flew up and hit her nose. Some fell down and started landing on her feet and nestled between her toes. The pop corn that fell on her lap was accumulating and in his mind he reached out and grabbed the popcorn and put it in his mouth. Mmmmmm. Tastes good. So, you get the idea? Imagine something funny, playful or simply outrageous. Above all think of something positive.

This is a pretty simplistic approach don't you think? You have to have a good imagination sometimes to get yourself out of these small irritations. Let me give you an example of a more serious deep rooted problem that occurred with Linda and me.

GREAT GRANDMA AT THE MEETING MOMENT

Linda and I went to a meeting together to hear about a particular software program. While at the meeting, the speaker said something to the effect that even a great grandma could operate this software. When he said that, I kind of chuckled and looked at Linda. She looked back at me and I smiled at her. At this point, Linda saw me as laughing at her. She said, "What are you thinking about, me?" I said, "Yes, you could even work this software." Linda replied sharply, "What's so funny about that? You are laughing at me and that's not funny! I don't see anything funny about that!" She said a few more things that were just not of her.

I could see that Satan had a hold of her again, playing on that weakness of not wanting to be looked at as being old. She is twenty three years old in her mind and she feels she stays young in mind and spirit because of this thinking. By the way, I think she is right! So, I see that Satan has a grip on her suggesting that she be offended at my chuckle about her being a great grandma working this software program. I felt prompted to say to her, "Calm down and don't be offended." in a serious tone. She came back with a comment that further caused me concern. Linda said sharply after sloughing off my comment, "Yeah, when someone is cutting you down how are you not supposed to be offended?"

This little discussion was going on while the speaker was still talking. I was holding her hand at the time and I was surprised that she continued to let me do so. I didn't hear anything more from her during the presentation. After the meeting was over, Linda and I had a chance to discuss what had happened and this is how it went.

After her last comment to me at the meeting, Linda closed her eyes. She felt Heavenly Father's spirit starting to dwell with her as she realized that she needed to do what I asked her to do. What I had said to her, "Calm down and don't be offended," brought back to her mind a commitment she had made to Heavenly Father. Linda had made the commitment to work on not becoming offended. This is an important point.

There are several ways to make a commitment. We can just say to ourselves that we are going to do a certain thing. A small commitment that we are likely to forget over time. We can make a commitment to someone else to do a certain thing. This is a much bigger commitment because then we have a witness that we have made this commitment. Also, this person can hold us accountable and remind us that we made this commitment.

The ultimate commitment is to make a promise or covenant with our Heavenly Father. This is witnessed by a heavenly host and God himself that you are willing to do what you say you are going to do. We are more likely to follow through with this type of commitment because it is so much more important and binding. I know that Heavenly Father will also bless us by being there for us. He will also be there for us to draw on Him in times of need. This is because we made a commitment with Him. Do you think He will let us down? I don't think so. As we make this strong commitment with Him, it will help us to remember it more so we will stick to it. I believe He will prompt us and help us like a friend to honor our commitment with Him. I highly suggest that when you are having trouble with a particular temptation or have a certain weakness that you make a commitment with our Heavenly Father to not do this thing. I know you will be stronger because of it through Him.

Linda had made such a commitment earlier in the week before this *moment* not to be offended. I think this is one of the most important commitments that someone can make in their life. Think about it. What is the most common thing in the world where Satan can get in and cause contention? I believe that being offended opens the door more to contention than anything else. Without someone being offended there would be no contention, right? A person has no reason to contend with someone else if there isn't a problem, right? Think about the last time or two when you had an argument or saw someone else having an argument. The thing that started the argument in the first place was that someone got offended, don't you agree?

There are many ways to get offended. Think about it. Ponder it. How many times have you been offended by someone else? What did they say or do to offend you? How could you have avoided being offended? You can not be offended unless you want to! Let me say that again. You can not be offended unless you want to. It's a choice. You get to choose to be offended or not to be offended at what people say or do. What's the old saying? Sticks and stones will break my bones but words will never harm me. The same goes for people's actions. Yes, people will be hurtful on purpose and on accident. It is how you choose to receive this hurtful or misguided action that will cause you to be offended or not. My challenge to you is to choose this day not to be offended. I have done it and so can you. I know you can do it.

Linda had made a commitment to Heavenly Father to work on not becoming offended recently. Satan knows of this commitment and is trying every which way at any time and any place to foil this commitment. So he whispers these nasty comments into her mind to be offended. As Linda described it, "Satan threw his fiery darts at me. It's like his darts pierced my skin, releasing a depressive toxin into my body. My body felt sick and depressed. Satan was suggesting that, *Kevan was belittling me and that I needed to get up and walk out. I didn't have to put up with someone treating me that way.*"

Heavenly Father to the rescue! I believe that I was prompted to lovingly tell her to calm down and not be offended. This was the first step of the help that she got from on high. A reminder through me from our Heavenly Father. The first step is to recognize that Satan was whispering to her. Linda closed her eyes and prayed to Heavenly Father to help her not be offended. Linda said, "I asked for power from on high to help me and all the while Satan was still piercing me with the fiery darts of negative thoughts. I kept praying and sincerely asked for help. Then I gradually rejected those darts that Satan was piercing me with." She began to have these thoughts come into her mind, "Kevan's heart is in the right place. He wouldn't purposely hurt me."

Linda continued, "Then I imagined an invisible sound proof bubble around Kevan as I reflected back upon his great grandma comments. Whatever he said to me, it's like I didn't hear it. It was like his laughter and words stayed within the bubble he was in. It didn't affect me at all. I kept feeling better and better." Then the spirit whispered to her, "Quickly forgive." Linda struggled with that for a moment and then she was prompted two more times to quickly forgive. Imagining talking to Father in Heaven she said in her mind quickly, "How can I?" Then she prayed some more. She felt so much better. Then the words of Pahoran in the *Book of Mormon*, Alma 61: 9, rang true in her ears, *it mattereth not*. These were the words Pahoran used after Moroni had chided him for not sending him the manpower he sorely needed to fight the Lamenites. Pahoran had troubles of his own with the Kingmen in Zarahemla and could not at that time send help to Moroni. He was in effect saying *it mattereth not* that Moroni was angry with him. He was not going to be angry back at Moroni for what harsh words Moroni had written to him. He rejoiced in the fact that Moroni had a good heart and that they were fighting for the same cause of liberty and freedom.

When these words came into Linda's mind, *it mattereth not*, she was freed from Satan and his influence. It mattereth not what Kevan did or said that could be construed as offending. The battle was over. What else could Satan do when it mattereth not? Just as Pahoran and Moroni were fighting for their freedom and liberty, so they came to fight for Linda to gain her freedom and liberty from Satan. Linda used many of the tools in her toolbox to get through this battle with Satan. I love the fact that Heavenly Father came to her rescue. If Linda had not been reading scriptures daily and refreshing her mind with these powerful words, she would not have been able to recognize what Heavenly Father was telling her through the promptings of the Holy Ghost, especially the part where Pahoran said, "It mattereth not."

This statement, it mattereth not, is so powerful. How many times do we have contention over things that mattereth not? There are things that we quibble over that mean absolutely nothing in this world that we esteem to be of great worth. We let Satan enter our lives in small and meaningless ways. You have to step back and look at why we are here. All these little things that we fight and argue over are meaningless dribble when you take into consideration the eternal purpose of why we are here.

Do you think it matters in the eternal scheme of things if I think something is funny and then Linda takes it wrong and gets upset and becomes offended? In this example, the part where I laughed does not matter in the least. The part where Linda would take it wrong and be offended does matter. The part that we all will be judged on is how we react or handle the situation.

This is more serious than most of us have ever thought. Not only do we jeopardize ourselves, but we also lead others down the path with us. It's not just you in the argument is it? It takes two to argue. When you get offended, what happens? You start saying angry and hurtful things to someone else so that they will get offended. You are *getting back* at them in a sense for offending you. You are influencing the other person to sin as well. Of course the other person does have the right to not become offended too. But many times the other person becomes drawn into the argument by Satan's design.

WORKING TOGETHER TO AVOID BEING OFFENDED

What about the offender? What I have talked about so far is about when your mate has said something unknowingly that you could take as offensive. Your mate didn't mean it that way but you took it that way. What if your mate said something to you that he or she knew was offensive? What if they just came in and started harshly yelling at you? What then? You still have the choice to be offended or not, don't you? What about them? They have a choice not to offend, but they are offending anyway, right? Again, you must use the tools in this book to diffuse an ugly situation. The offender must recognize what they are doing. How do they do that? You must help them to recognize what they are doing by using the stop stop stop tool. Put your hand up with the palm toward them and say, "Stop stop stop," in a calm voice. Then say to them, "How could you say that differently?" Help them to see what they are doing.

There is no reason that anything should be discussed when someone is yelling or highly emotionally negatively charged. You must help your mate to see that what they are doing is destructive and unproductive. Satan is leading them down a path that will only hurt their relationship. Until they become calm and Satan can be cast out, there is no use in discussing anything. Set this up ahead of time with your mate.

Agree ahead of time what each of you will do if a situation arises like this one in the future. Then abide by those terms. A set of terms might look like this. When your mate puts their hand up and says' "Stop stop stop," you will stop immediately and take stock of what you are doing. You are doing something wrong. When they say, "How could you say that differently," stop and think of how you could be more positive with your last statement. If they ask you to cast Satan out, do it now without hesitation. When you cast Satan out, do it with faith and conviction. If you set up an agreement like this ahead of time and stick to it, you will find that you can calm down and discuss something without being offensive.

Do you want a great way to diffuse an argument before it happens? Ok, here is the big secret. Don't argue. "Oh brother," you say. It's not that simple is it? Yes, I believe it is. I practice it right now. I have practiced it ever since an event in my life I call the phone throwing event which I will describe just a little later. For now, let's just say that I have made my mind up not to argue or raise my voice. It is a conscious effort on my part that first, I will not get offended and second, since I am not offended there is nothing to argue about. Do you see what I mean? There is one more trick. Ahhhhh, you knew there had to be another trick right? Well this really isn't a trick, but it works.

I also do not always have to be right. I can be wrong and it is alright. I mess up sometimes or am not correct about all things. I can also agree to disagree. You have the right to your opinion and so do I. We don't have to convince each other. Keeping in mind these three things, not to be offended, I don't have to be right, and I can agree to disagree, will keep you from arguing. Linda and I have never argued and never will. While at least one of you is very staunch and set on not arguing with the preceding parameters, there can't be an argument. One cannot argue with a stone wall. It really comes down to not being offended in most cases.

There is one more factor to consider. Have you ever been in a discussion or argument and as you proceeded to talk about the matter, you suddenly realized that what the other person was saying made sense to you? You thought to yourself, "They are correct and I am wrong. But I can't give in now, I would look foolish. I have to continue as if I am right." Have you ever had thoughts like that? Some people, even after knowing they are wrong, will continue with their line of thinking because of pride. Yes, you know what I am talking about, don't you? It's flat out pride that won't let you admit that you are wrong. You won't admit that the other person is right. Satan loves to see your pride get in your way. Satan whispers to you, *"Don't give in. Who cares if they are right. You have to stick up for yourself. You have to win at all costs or you will look bad. You don't want to look bad in front of them do you?"* You must fight off these demonic suggestions and stop what you are doing. Admit that the other person is right. It's ok to be wrong and admit it. Say something like, "I see your point. You have convinced me that what you say is valid." End your pride now and you will see peace restored to your household. Remember, you are being honest with your mate and by holding onto your pride; you are being dishonest by not admitting they are right. So, release that pride because it's OK if you are not always right.

Being Offended Is A Waste Of Time

Being offended is also a waste of time and energy. The act of not getting offended is a huge time saver and eliminates contention. Let's take the extreme example of what happens to a person when they become offended. Ok, John is offended by his neighbor over some property dispute. They argue over this time and time again. John has harbored evil thoughts toward his neighbor for years. John is always thinking of how he can get back at him. He devises a plan and puts it into action. "Hooray," he shouts, "I put him in his place!" Then his neighbor devises a plan to get back at John. And John gets it put back to him by his neighbor. This goes back and forth until it finally gets to a point where John gets so mad he ends up killing his neighbor. John spends years and years in prison for his act. He also looses the property that was under dispute in the first place.

Yes, this is an extreme case and something with which I am sure that you as a reader are not familiar with on a personal level. The point is this. Look at all the time that was devoted to tearing down someone else. Time was spent on thought to devise retaliation on the neighbor. The time put into action to carry out the plan. And the time spent in prison speaks for itself, not to mention all the money that it cost for defense and the loss of the land that was in dispute and maybe more. There may have been family members that were involved that were also affected. I am sure there are many other aspects involved with this story that could fill an entire book, but you get the point. Look at all the time and energy that was put into evil! We will be judged on all that. John could have avoided all of that time and energy spent on this dispute by being not offended. If he would have gone to his neighbor and settled the dispute, even if he gave up everything that was being disputed, he would have been much better off, don't you agree?

You say, "Yeah, with 20/20 hindsight I can see this." Why can't we see this for what it is? It is Satan whispering to us day and night to prod us on to be offended. Then he continues to push harder and harder to be offended even more. It is a battle against Satan that we don't recognize here, not the battle with our neighbor. Forgive our neighbor. Stop the fight. It's a waist of time and energy that could be put toward good works. If you want to fight, fight against Satan and his angels. That's a fight worth fighting against.

Fight those evil thoughts. If you don't, those evil thoughts will be turned into action. This action is surely turned into causing contention and being offended and on and on from there down the spiral staircase to destruction. Do you get the point I am making here? Stop! Stop Satan from the beginning. It doesn't matter how far it could have gone or what your intentions were at the beginning. You don't intend to take an argument any further than arguing right? That's one of the biggest lies Satan wants you to believe. You can control yourself right? When you get caught up in emotion and your feelings have been hurt and you are offended, look out, anything can happen. I know, I have been there. I don't ever want that to happen to me again.

OUT OF CONTROL

I am a very docile low key laid back kind of guy generally. It takes a lot to get me riled up. I remember talking to my soon to be ex wife on the phone. We were talking about the settlement between us. I don't remember the whole conversation, I only remember that I felt she was being very unreasonable in splitting up our assets. I was getting so angry I was screaming into the phone. When I hung up from that conversation I was so angry I threw the cordless phone across the room.

This was so unlike me. I am not a violent person. I was doing just what Satan wanted me to do. He wants all of us to *get out of control*. As he whispers to us and coaxes us to get angry and say things that we really don't mean to hurt someone else, he is leading us down the path of destruction.

"And there are also secret combinations, even as in times of old, according to the combinations of the devil, for he is the founder of all these things; yea, the founder of murder, and works of darkness; yea, and he leadeth them by the neck with a flaxen cord, until he bindeth them with his strong cords forever." (*Book of Mormon*, 2Nephi 26: 22)

I was being led by the flaxen cord (a small thread) little by little as I got angrier until the flaxen cord turned into ropes pulling me along. Pulling me until the fit of rage got *out of control* where I was led to do a violent action, throwing the phone. You see, the more you allow yourself to be led by Satan on his side of the line, the more power he has to influence you.

It's like a ball sitting on top of a hill. A line is drawn on the very peak of the hill to divide the left from the right. You are the ball on the top of the hill. On the left side of the line the hill slopes downward toward Satan. On the right side of the line the hill slopes downward toward Heavenly Father. As Satan whispers negative thoughts and half truths to your mind you start to believe them. At that point, the ball (you), starts rolling down the left side of the hill towards Satan. The more you get down the hill the faster you pick up speed. The more speed you pickup the more influence Satan has over you. That is because it is easier to keep the ball rolling than it is to stop it. Once you get offended and Satan influences you to get angry about it, he has more impact on you to push you further down his side of the hill. Like the ball rolling downhill, it doesn't take much effort to keep the ball rolling, does it?

Let's just say that you recognize that you are rolling down Satan's side of the hill and you stop. That is the first step. Now, Satan doesn't want you to stop. So sometimes it takes a bit of effort to get that ball stopped and rolling up hill to the top so that you can get back over to Heavenly Fathers side of the hill. This is where *How To Build Marriage Unity That Will Endure Throughout All Eternity* comes in. You need to use the tools presented in this book to push the ball (you) back up the hill and get you to the other side. Once you do get onto the other side, the Lords side, try to get as far down the hill as possible. Remember, the further down the hill and the faster you go the less likely you are to be pulled up the hill and to the other side. You get down the Lord's side by praying, reading scriptures, not being offended, thinking positive thoughts, and tons of other tools that are in these fine pages.

Now, back to what happened to me after the phone throwing event. Satan had me in such a rage that I couldn't sleep that night. At this point in my life I had no idea that Satan was influencing me to go down this path. I was not privy to all the information I have today. It so happened, it was Saturday night when this dreadful event happened. I went to church the next day feeling down and depressed. In one of the classes, the subject under discussion was about the following:

> "And if any man will sue thee at the law, and take away thy coat, let him have thy cloke also." (*Bible*, King James Version, Mathew 5: 40)

It hit me like a ton of bricks. I knew what I had to do. That evening I called my soon to be ex wife and told her that I was sorry for yelling at her and that she could divide up our assets however she wanted and that I would agree to it. I knew that the division of assets would be in her favor and that I would get less than I deserved, but suddenly I felt better about the whole thing. I chose not to argue or be offended. I chose to forgive and I let it go. The anger was gone and I felt so much better. I knew I did the right thing. From that time on I chose not to be offended or argue with anyone. "No matter what happened to me, I will not be offended or argue." is what I said. I had stopped my ball and had rolled it to the right side, the Lord's side of the hill. From that point on I have not argued or allowed myself to be offended by anyone.

CHOOSE THIS DAY NOT TO BE OFFENDED

Linda and I were having dinner with a couple of friends. We were discussing this topic of not being offended. The fellow looked over at me after we had discussed this for a while and said, "I can see that in you. I can see how you could be that way, but I have a different personality. I don't think I can do it like you can." Whoa Nelly Bells! Hold the horses! I thought to myself, "So you think that you haven't got the choice to choose not to be offended?" We were all put on this earth with the ability to make a decision. It's called free agency right? If you don't think you can do something like choosing not to be offended, who do you think put that into your mind, huh? Who chose the plan of compulsion? Who does not want you to have freedom of choice? Satan of course! He wants us to believe we can't do something positive like choosing not to be offended. I am offended by his comment! Ha ha, not really, because I choose not to be offended and I am committed to that.

Not becoming offended was not easy for me to do at first. As I worked at it, it became easier and easier to control my emotions. I just kept these thoughts in my mind, "Whatever happens to me just is. Whenever someone says something negative to me, that's just the way they are and I can't change that. I can't control them. I can only change the way I feel about what happens to me. I choose not to be offended or affected."

I also had met a man at that time that was going through a rough time and I had seen his wife yell and scream at him about things and yet he did not raise his voice to her. We talked about it later and he told me he had made a choice not to raise his voice. He said his parents always yelled and screamed at each other and he thought that was wrong. He made a commitment to himself that he would not raise his voice to anyone. I admired that in him and decided that if he could do it, I could do the same.

No matter what your personality is, you have a choice. You may be of the type that gets offended easily and have all your life. I didn't say it would be easy if this is your personality. It will take work on your part. You have to recognize those negative feelings and purge them from your very being. Use the scripture about Pahoran in the *Book of Mormon* I talked about earlier. *It mattereth not* what people say or do to you. It mattereth what you do with what they say or do. It's not what happens to us that makes us mad or angry, it's what we do with it when it happens. No one can make us do anything. It is our perception of what happened and it is our reality what we do with it that will determine how we feel about it. In other words, if we take the attitude that it mattereth not, it won't have any impact on us. It just is.

It just is, is something that should be an automatic response in your head when something negative happens to you or is said to you. Give it no emotion. It will have power over you if you assign it an emotion. Satan loves that when he can see that you are getting angry or upset about something. It gives him a chance to whisper a bunch of stuff that will cause you to get more upset and angry. When Satan sees a sore, he will get in there and pour lemon juice on it at first to get it to sting real bad. As you get more upset about the sting he will pour acid on the wound and get you real wound up. Thoughts of anger and revenge will cloud your mind. Then he has you where he wants you. Don't give him that honor. You are stronger than Satan! You have the tools. You know how to use them. Get in that toolbox and get out the spiritual tools you need. Use the scripture tool right now by saying, "It mattereth not."

It Mattereth Not

I have said it mattereth not a number of times within these passages. What exactly does that mean? Does it mean that nothing matters? No, I don't think so. It means that most stuff in this world really isn't worth fighting over and getting upset over when you put it in perspective with why we are here. Do you think it will matter in the eternities and to our salvation that your spouse was running behind in getting ready and it made the two of you late for a meeting? Would it matter in the eternities if your spouse said something that embarrassed you in front of a lot of people? Would it matter if someone laughed at you because you were a great grandma even though you felt younger? None of these things are that important to what really matters. They are only a moment in time. A very small moment in time compared to the eternities. It may seem long to us right now as we go through this life, but we need to keep in mind the reason we are here. We are here to work out our own salvation.

Believe me when I say, you will be thankful that if you chose not to be offended, though hard it may seem, your life will never be the same. This is a huge step in having a little heaven here on earth. Once you have experienced it you will never turn back. Work on choosing not to be offended with your spouse. Help each other recognize early if one of you is offended and then help them to correct it in a loving manner.

Not being offended is at the center of all relationships. This includes the relationship with our Heavenly Father. I believe that *all* relationships hang on five primary principals. Honesty, unconditional love, forgiveness, unselfishness and not being offended are five of the key factors in making a happy relationship. For now, let's talk about not being offended. I believe that if at least one of you has as his or her anchor, not being offended, that your relationship will not go adrift. If one of you is grounded as to not be offended, you can help the other recognize and get over being offended as well. This key ingredient if integrated in your life I believe is one of the largest corner stones and foundation builders of your marriage. As I said earlier, if one of you is offended and the other is not, it is impossible to have an argument. This is because as the one who is offended is getting upset and saying things to the other who cannot be offended, the not offended person will not say anything negative back to the other. This will end the conversation. But, the real objective of the not offended person should be to get the offended person to recognize what is happening and to use the tools outlined herein to help them not be offended.

So what am I saying with all these experiences? I think that at the root of almost every contention and argument, Satan is there whispering to us to be offended. One of his biggest objectives is to influence us to be offended by what people say or do to us. Life is not perfect. At some time or another someone will make a comment or do something that is offensive. Guaranteed! And yet, you do not have to take offense. It is your choice to be offended or not.

Choose this day not to be offended. Make a promise to the Lord that you will not be offended and keep that commitment and promise. Keep *How To Build Marriage Unity That Will Endure Throughout All Eternity* handy so that you will be able to use the tools to help you and your spouse to stay on the Lords side of the hill and teach other people what you have learned. In that way we can all look out for each other. Focus on your spouse to help each other with these tools. Work on not being offended and you will see a big change in your life. You will be so much happier and have less stress in your life. You and your mate can help each other greatly and as you work as a team to improve your ability to not become offended and as you do so, you will become a great strength together.

Helpful Tools Identified
Or Explained In This Chapter:

1. We have free agency to choose not to become offended.
2. Look and listen for something positive to focus on if you feel like you are becoming offended.
3. Make a commitment to Heavenly Father to work on not becoming offended.
4. Recognize Satan's whispering to you or your spouse.
5. Pray for help to not become offended.
6. Liken the scriptures to you to strengthen you.
7. Use the, *it mattereth not* tool.
8. Read scriptures daily.
9. Recognize the promptings of Heavenly Father through the Holy Ghost.
10. Remember our eternal purpose and why we are here.
11. Don't argue. Be a brick wall if you have to but say nothing to escalate a heated conversation.
12. Use the *stop stop stop* tool.
13. Use the *how could you say that differently* tool.
14. Cast Satan out with faith and conviction.
15. You don't have to be right.
16. You can agree to disagree.
17. When you recognize that the other person is right, acknowledge it and move on.
18. Forgive and let it go.
19. Think positive thoughts.
20. Free agency.
21. Use the, *it just is* tool.
22. Choose not to raise your voice in anger.
23. Recognize the negative feelings that you have and purge them from your very being.
24. Give it no emotion.

8

IT JUST IS.

Have you ever wondered why your mate does things a certain way? Have you ever wondered why they can't do it *your way*? Have you ever thought that you could tell your mate a better way to do something? Have you ever wondered why your spouse insists on doing it their way? Of course you have thought these thoughts. If you are human, you can't help but think thoughts like this. Each of us is different and thinks and does things differently.

I used to ask myself questions like that. I used to think that way. I don't anymore because this is self defeating. It takes time and energy to think about something that just is. Some people are really focused on changing the other person. Don't confuse changing the other person with helping them to overcome their weaknesses and the temptations of Satan. Some people think that they would be so much happier if their spouse did this certain thing that way instead of this way. They really work on trying to get their mate to conform to the way they want it. I am not saying that this is a bad thing, but it can be taken to extreme.

Let's say for example, Jim comes in the house during a rain storm and doesn't take his boots off before coming into the house. He walks in with mud on his boots and tracks through the living room. Sarah gets after Jim and scolds him about taking his boots off at the door so he doesn't track through the house. She is trying to train Jim to take off his boots so he doesn't get the house dirty. This is a logical and worthy goal and perfectly understandable.

The extreme might be that Sarah wants Jim to always take off his boots whether it's raining or not. Then put his boots in a plastic bag and carry them with two hands while he walks only on the left hand side of the room (not in the middle of the room), down the hall to the closet where he puts the shoe bag on a designated shelf. He then has to get the vacuum out and vacuum where he had just walked. After the vacuuming, take out the bag and replace it with a new one. Then get a dust rag and polish the vacuum before putting it away. Then rinsing out the dust rag and put it into the laundry room. If Jim doesn't do this prescribed procedure with exact precision and Sarah finds out, look out! Sarah may blow her top because she has told Jim a hundred times how to do this. OK, yes this is extremely extreme, but I think you get the point, or do you?

When is a good time for *training* and when is a good time to let it go? Sometimes this is a little bit of a grey area. This will be something that you will have to discuss with your eternal companion. There are certain habits that your mate has done for years. You aren't going to change that habit for all the tea in China, right? So stop trying. Instead, ask your spouse about the habit that annoys you so much. Ask them why they do a certain thing a certain way. Try to understand their thinking instead of trying to pressure them into just doing it your way.

You can express for example that your way could be more logical or practical, but if what your spouse is doing fits their needs better than logical or practical, accept it and move on. No one should be forced to do anything. God put us on this earth with free agency. To force someone to do something your way either through physical, mental or emotional means would be going against the principles of God. If there is a good reason that your mate is doing something a certain way and it works for them, let them do it their way and accept it. It just is. The more you accept things in your life and remember that it just is, the more you will have peace in your life. You will not be constantly worrying and fretting about what other people are doing.

Here is an example: I have an office that I work in with all kinds of paperwork. A lot of the time I prepare papers, bills, packages, or have other things I need to take with me when I leave the house. I have a filing system for this stuff on the floor of my office by the door. Anything I need to take with me I put by the door on the floor. I do this so that I will see it before I leave and it will remind me to take it with me. I have done this for years and it is a good system for me. Linda on the other hand does not like that I leave this stuff on the floor where someone could step on it or trip over it. If it were up to her, she would have me pick the stuff up and move it somewhere else. She would want me to pick a new place for my stuff. We have talked about this together and she has decided to accept what is. This is the way I do it. She realizes that this is a system that has worked for me for so many years and is willing to forgo her feeling about it to make me happy. Once the decision was made, nothing more has been said about it. Linda has accepted that it just is!

Look around at what your mate does that bugs you a little or maybe a lot. You have probably tried to train your spouse to do something different without success. Some things are engrained so deeply that there is no changing that person's habit, unless they want to. I know this book is all about changing your bad habits into good habits, but some things can be left unchanged. Those things that really don't mean a hill of beans can be accepted for what they are. It just is. Give no feeling or emotion to it. By doing so you are respecting your mate and the way they do things. You will be showing forth unconditional love if you accept the way they do things.

Really, if you look at it, nothing should come between you and your eternal companion. You should ask yourself, "Is what I am trying to change in my spouse going to drive a wedge between us? Is it worth the contention for me to insist on my mate to do it my way?" You see what I am getting at, don't you? Of course you do.

So the next step, once you accept what is, is for you to stop thinking about it! That's right. Accept it and move on. Don't give it another thought! If you think about it each time you see your mate doing the thing that you want them to do your way, it will irritate you and irritate you until you can't stand it anymore. You will simply blow up one day. Let it go. Accept what is and move on. Love your mate unconditionally.

So, what have you learned in this chapter? There are many things that we need to change in our lives to make them better and to create harmony with our spouse, but some things should be thought of as *it just is*. If something bothers you about your mate, if you can just rearrange your thinking a little and accept what just is, you would be much better off. If it is something that you just can't live with, then discuss it with your mate and come up with a solution. Don't say, "I can't live with this or that." just because you want your way. Allow your eternal mate the freedom to be who he or she really is as much as possible. Keep in mind that you are both working on being the eternal couple. Let go of the things that bother you that don't really matter in the eternal scheme of things. Release your thoughts about what was bugging you and let it go. Whatever you do, don't nag your mate about anything. Speak kindly to one another and emphasize the good in one another. You will get more positive action with compliments than with derogatory remarks.

If you are truly trying to get good at applying the principles in this book, you will succeed at accomplishing your goal. You cannot fail! The only way you will fail is if you stop trying. You are simply taking one step at a time toward perfection. Continue to work with your eternal mate. Continue to use the tools you have learned about in this book and you and your eternal mate will become a great strength together.

Helpful Tools Identified Or Explained In This Chapter:

1. It just is.
2. Let it go.
3. Free agency.
4. Accept what just is.
5. Give no feeling or emotion to it.
6. Unconditional love.
7. Once you accept what is, stop thinking about it.
8. Speak kindly to one another.
9. Emphasize the good in one another.
10. Compliments.

9

SATAN'S TACTIC; LINKING AND YOUR PERCEPTIONS

Satan has a way of linking events and thoughts together to continually draw us back to a dark and dreary cave where he can inflict more pain upon you. His fiery darts are striking us with more intensity. They are accumulating into a huge bonfire with which he hopes will consume us. This linking or connecting of events and thoughts is very convincing to our minds that a misconception or half truth is true. He plays on our weaknesses and fears to bring us to a boiling point that will hopefully send us out of control. His whisperings are carefully crafted to hit us at our weak points where we are most vulnerable to accept these as our own thoughts. These half truths seem so real to us as he builds upon them one straw at a time until the back of the camel is broken.

The truth of the matter is that most of the time these half truths are based on a misperception. What I am talking about is that everyone has their own point of view, right? Each of us sees things through our own eyes and thinks differently. We have our own ideas and ways of doing things. We also have different reasons for why we do things in a certain way. My perception may or may not be different from yours even if we are doing the same thing right beside each other. We see things through different filters if you will.

Each of us has filters that we use to determine what information will be useful to us. These filters have been created from our past experiences and beliefs. We collect information through our five senses and beyond. It may be from seeing, hearing, feeling, tasting, smelling or a combination of these senses. By using these senses as we go through our different experiences in life, we set a program within ourselves to filter out or accept certain things. We actually program ourselves much like a computer program.

Let's take Microsoft Word for example. It is programmed, as you type on the computer, to accept correctly spelled words and to underline in red the words that are misspelled. Isn't that great! It keeps you from misspelling words by alerting you with the red underlining. So, how do you think it knows what is wrong or right? It had to be programmed by someone with the correct words, right? This was what the computer program experienced.

What if you typed in the word thinketh? I guarantee it will underline it in red to say you spelled it wrong. It filtered the word through its logic and experience and said it's misspelled. Now, I know you have seen this word in the scriptures, so you know it is spelled correctly. But, the computer hasn't *experienced* this word before so through it's perception, it thinks it is wrong. So, all you have to do to correct the misperception that the computer program has, is to fix the problem, right? You just have to do a spell check. The computer finds the word thinketh and asks you to correct it. It even gives you possible alternatives. You, knowing it is spelled correctly, click on the, *add to dictionary* button. You now have changed the computers programming through this experience, which has changed it's perception of what is now correct. Through this experience, the computer program is now ready to accept the new perception that this word when typed into the program is a correctly spelled word.

THE BOILING EGG MOMENT

I am going to relate a few stories to illustrate how this works in everyday simple living and conversations. Linda was boiling some eggs one day. She had put them on the stove, turned on the heat and went into her office to do some work. I had been gone from home for a while and upon my returning I walked past the stove and noticed that the water in the pan of boiling eggs was almost gone. I turned the burner off and went into Linda's office and said in what I thought was a playful tone, "How long have you been boiling those eggs? They are done now." Linda heard it in her mind as if I said this comment in a serious tone. At that moment, Satan whispered to Linda, "*There he goes again. He is trying to control you!*"

A little background on Linda is what is needed to get the full impact of this story. Just like the computer program described earlier, Linda has had certain programming in her life. Linda grew up in an environment with a very controlling father. She saw the impact that had on her mother and family. This programmed her to resent anyone from controlling her. In fact, in the past, she would get really offended and would lash out at someone who would try to control her. She would actually do the opposite of what someone would want her to do whether it was in her best interest or not. Satan really had hold of her and actually had great influence over her. At the time, she didn't know that Satan had so much influence over her. Satan knows what our weaknesses are and will exploit them faster than a speeding bullet. Therefore, he was whispering to Linda to be offended and to take my comment wrong.

Six days before this moment, Linda had made a commitment to God that she would work on not becoming offended. The anger started to rise within her after I had made this comment to her. Thoughts of retaliation came into her mind as they had in the past. She realized that these were negative thoughts and remembering that she made a promise to Heavenly Father to work on not becoming offended, she chose not to retaliate or be offended. Linda decided to be a little silly instead. She said, "The eggs have been boiling for about ten and three quarters of thirty seven seconds of an hour." I said, "OK", and we both laughed at that silly comment. What kind of time is that?

As we talked about this situation later Linda said to me, "Grant you, it takes a lot of conscious effort on my part to recognize that those negative thoughts were coming from Satan and not to give in. Because of the whisperings of Satan, your comment seemed much more extreme than it really was. I recognized my weakness that when I feel someone is trying to control me I lash out. This is something I am working on and it isn't easy. But, in this instance I was victorious."

Linda's programmed perception through Satan's whisperings was that I was being controlling. My perception was that I was informing her that the eggs were done. We both were sifting the event through our own personal filters or programming. You get the point?

As you probably noticed, Satan was linking back to Linda's childhood as he puts thoughts into her mind about being controlled. Actually, every incident in her life from childhood to adulthood, Satan has been linking one event after another. He has been building one event on top of another until hundreds of events have, "*made us the way we are.*" We tend to buy into this myth quite readily. Most of us do not realize that Satan is behind all this madness. Satan assists you to believe that these events that he has carefully crafted are of you. He convinces you that the thoughts and reactions you had about these experiences are from you. Then once you believe that it is you, it becomes you. It is you because you own it. Therefore, since you believe it is a part of you, you can't change it. He makes you feel that you haven't got a choice. "*That's just the way you are.*" Satan whispers.

Satan links all of our perceptions and misperceptions together into one big lie. The lie is that we can not change our circumstances or have any choice of how we react to them. Of course we cannot change the past but we can change the way we feel about what happened. We can change the way we feel about what happens to us now. Remember, you have a choice. It is not what happens to us that makes us who we are, it is how we think and react to what happens to us that determines who we will become.

Think about that for a moment. It is not what happens to us, it is how we take what happens and what we do with it that shapes our character and our life. We are so much more than we think we are. We are so much more capable and have so much more potential than we realize. We can all take what happens to us and turn it around into something positive. We just have to practice it until we become good at it. Ok, enough said, on to the next link!

THE TEMPERATURE MOMENT

Living here in Arizona the weather can be quite extreme. It is summer now and it can be quite hot. Almost every day we check the temperature and inform one another how hot the morning is. On this particular morning, Linda went outside to check out how the weather felt. She came back in and said to me, "It does feel a lot cooler outside this morning." I said to her, "What's the temperature?" Linda replied, "I don't know." I retorted, "You mean you walked by the temperature gauge and you didn't even check it?" I said that in an astonished type of tone because for the past few weeks she has always checked the temperature and came and told me the number. Linda felt in her mind that I said it in an authoritative voice as if to say, "Well, I can't believe you didn't even check the temperature." as if to put her down.

You see how that each of our minds *filter* the statement that I made? I thought I used an astonished tone and she thought it was authoritative and degrading. Well, Satan took advantage of this moment to interject something into Linda's mind. He said, "*Kevan is being controlling. He is cutting you down and chiding you.*" As Linda, recognized those feelings that stirred up inside of her as being negative, she felt she better diffuse the situation before she blew up. She said to me in a kidding way, "You mean you didn't check the temperature gauge when you went outside?" I told her that I had just looked out the back door and there was no temperature gauge there. Linda, again in her playful way said, "You mean you wanted to know what the temperature was and you didn't even go and check it?"

I could see what was happening here. Even though the situation wasn't totally going negative, I could see that Linda was stressing over this situation. She was being playful in the way she was stating her comments, but again, it seemed so unlike her. I could see her struggling with something. I decided to diffuse what was happening by taking her by the arm and saying, "Let's go check the temperature." Linda smiled and said, "Yes, let's do it together." We both ran over to the temperature gauge to see what it was. We laughed as we ran. This is an action that we often do together because it does make us laugh. Sometimes we chase each other around the house or run from one room to another to see who can get there first just for fun. In this case, it relieved what tension there was and by laughing, Satan's whisperings of me controlling and cutting Linda down were flattened.

This worked for the time being, but an hour later Satan was back in there trying to wedge his way into Linda's mind again. Thoughts came streaming in saying, "*Kevan is controlling and cutting you down.*" Satan again was *linking* to the previous day about the egg boiling moment. See how he builds a case of negativity towards the other spouse? This was frustrating Linda because these thoughts kept coming into her mind. This is the third time these thoughts had come into her mind about the same thing. She had battled Satan twice before and was able to get through it without creating an incident. Linda at this point was starting to feel bad and was starting to give into these whisperings. Then she thought, "Help! Satan is starting to break down my spirit! I need to repair my spirit. I need to tune it up! I am getting out *How To Build Marriage Unity That Will Endure Throughout All Eternity* now!" She read down the list of tools and picked out a couple of them and used them. She was finally able to get those thoughts out of her mind.

THE LAUNDRY MOMENT

The next day, Linda was washing the laundry. I was working on a project on the house and was going back and forth to the garage and through the laundry room. As I was going back and forth I would notice that the washer and dryer had stopped. The loads of laundry needed to be switched around. Linda's office where she was working was also on my way to the garage. That morning, I had told her two different times that the washer and dryer had stopped. The reason I reminded her was because of my own forgetfulness when I have done laundry in the past. I usually get busy doing something and the whole day will slip by before I remember about changing around the laundry.

Linda's perception on being reminded is that she is an adult and is capable of doing the laundry without being reminded or told what to do as the process moves along. She looked at me as being controlling or nagging. In the past, Linda would have told me to do my own laundry and she will do hers if I don't like the way she was doing it. She would also have said some other negative things that could have hurt me and would have surely regretted them later. Since Linda's commitment to God and to me that she will work on not becoming offended, she reached into *How To Build Marriage Unity That Will Endure Throughout All Eternity* and got to work on not becoming offended.

Satan was at work whispering the same thing he had been whispering over the last couple of days, "*Kevan is being controlling.*" Satan has been building each day upon the same weakness that Linda has. Those fiery darts were getting more and more intense trying to build up the bonfire of emotion to flame up within Linda. Although my intention was not to be controlling, that emotion in Linda is what Satan was playing on to get her riled up.

Linda reached into this book and took out this tool: I will not give any thought or feeling to Kevan's comments. The other tool she used was to let it go. Let go of blame and judgment. As Linda thought of these two tools she was able to reverse any negative thoughts she had, giving no thought or feeling to it and letting it go. Linda admits that this was not easy but she concentrated on doing what she knew to be right. This was another victory over Satan for her.

Each of our filters was sifting the information from past experiences to give us a certain outcome. For me, my filter was telling me that I should remind Linda about the laundry because that has been a weakness for me in the past. Sometimes I need to be reminded and that doesn't bother me. Therefore my filter tells me that if I am weak in that area, maybe Linda might be weak there too. In this case, this is a misperception on my part. I also made the mistake to "assume" that she was like me. But that's another issue.

Linda's filter gave her yet another perception. She looked at what I had done as being controlling because she could take care of the laundry herself. On both of our parts, there were misperceptions. We each thought something different about the motives of the other. We needed to clear these misperceptions to help us move forward and to not carry any negative thoughts with us. This is where, like the computer when you push the, *add to dictionary* button, you have the chance to correct the misperception.

As I approached Linda later on, we began to discuss the matter openly. We did this by talking to one another to find out what each others motives actually were. This will give you understanding of your spouses thinking and intentions. Here again, be honest and tell it like it is, positive or negative so that all is worked out. Then, come up with a solution. How will you handle this in the future? Every time you talk about and resolve a certain situation, the next time this issue comes up, you will know how to handle it. Eventually, you will have a solution for almost all the possible situations that may arise.

Learn To Recognize The Links

These are not just stories that I am relating to you. These are real life situations that actually took place. Do you see how Satan is trying to weave his lies and half truths within our lives? Do you see how our own personal filters can cause misperceptions in our interaction with others? I am sure you are aware of these things and how Satan has disrupted your life. You have been in similar situations where Satan has whispered things to you to believe certain things that really weren't true. The point here is to recognize these patterns that Satan is weaving. Recognize the connection of Satan's lies from one situation to another. Recognize the linking of these misguided thoughts that are negative. Recognize these ugly vicious lies that play on our weaknesses and stir up the emotion within us. Learn to recognize these whisperings for what they are. Satan and his demonic spirits are trying to split you up, the celestial couple.

Remember that it is not what happens to us that makes us who we are, it is how we think and react to what happens to us that determines who we will become. You have a choice. Choose how to feel when something negative happens to you or something is said to you that could be taken negatively. Be better than you are now by reacting positively and not being offended. Take control of you and the things that you can control and don't worry about the things you can't control. Use this book to help you get through life's challenges.

Just like the computer program that recognizes incorrectly spelled words because of its filters, we must recognize the negative promptings from Satan. Recognize that we all use our filters to sift the incoming information from an event or conversation. We have our own perceptions of what reality is.

Remember that you have control over what you think and react to when negative situations arise. Just like you have control over the keyboard to type in whatever you choose in the computer program. You may need to make corrections to your programming from time to time. Just as you can add a word to the dictionary to correct the computers misperception of a word you know is spelled correctly, you can change your misperception of an event or conversation by talking it over with your spouse and clearing it up. It is imperative for you to do this so that you don't bring any baggage with you. Satan loves linking all this negative stuff together and it is your job to break the link. Stop lugging all the baggage around.

Just as the computer is now set up to recognize the new word you put into it as being spelled correctly, you and your spouse will set up a way to handle that situation should it arise in the future.

THE TOOL POUCH MOMENT

One more story about perception. Linda and I were talking one day about Linda needing some tools to finish a project she was working on. I was willing to help with getting her the tools she needed. I said, "My tool pouch is out in the garage hanging on the right side of the cabinets. Linda said "It's always been on the left. Did you move it?" I said, "No, the tools have always been in the same place." "So the tools are on the left side then." retorted Linda. I looked at her and replied, "As you look at the cabinets, the tool pouch is on the right." Linda looked puzzled while she said, "If the tools are where they have always been, then they are on the left." Have you ever had a discussion like this one? Linda thinks the tool pouch is on the left and I think it's on the right.

Each person is insistent that they are correct in their thinking. This is such a simple thing that could possibly get out of hand. Each person knows that their perception is true and wanting to persuade the other to believe what they are saying. Can they both be right? Can the tools be on the left and on the right? Let's find out what happened.

At this point, Linda and I went out into the garage to see where the tool pouch was. As we walked out into the garage, the cabinets (as I called them were actually shelves) were on the left hand side of the garage. Linda pointed this out to me by standing at the door of the garage and showing me as she said, "See, the tool pouch is on the left side." I looked at the shelves and hanging there on the right side of the shelving was the tool pouch. Linda was correct in thinking that the tool pouch was on the left side of the garage and yet I was correct in thinking that they were on the right side of the shelving.

As you can see, our perceptions were different in the way we looked at what we were describing. I think this is pretty common among couples who are communicating with each other. Several things happened here. First, I was not as clear as I should have been when I said that the tool pouch was on the right side of the cabinets. This flew right over Linda's head because she knew there were no cabinets in the garage. She didn't understand that I was really referring to the shelving. Also, Linda thinks in more broad terms than I do so she was thinking, *left side of the garage.* I am more of a detail person, so my thinking went past just being in the garage and directly to the shelving where in my mind I could see the tool pouch hanging on the right side of the shelves.

I think this is a typical miscommunication scenario that most couples go through. Have you ever been in a conversation where you said something that your spouse misinterpreted? They took what you said and started down a new path and line of reasoning. Then as you tried to correct that misinterpretation, the conversation only got worse. I know you have been there and you know what I am talking about.

These kinds of conversations generally turn into arguments because it gets so far off track from the original conversation that you can't come back to it. The conversation gets so splintered that the only way to get back to the original conversation is to stop your current conversation and start over. Sometimes that is impossible because of what was said in the splintered conversations. Then if that doesn't start you arguing then

Satan has one more tactic to get you going. It's called she said he said. This is very dangerous territory if you don't handle it right.

This is where you try to resolve what was said and try to understand why your spouse said a certain thing. He said that he said a certain thing based on what she said. Then she says, "Well, because you said this, I said that." "Once you said that, then I had to say blah blah blah etc." Then you argue about who said what and analyze the reasons you said what you said and how you should have said something else and how could you even think that, etc. Have you ever done that? Have you ever tried to work out a solution by going over what you just argued about to see what happened so that you can avoid the same thing in the future? And then you argue about it again? Satan loves to see this kind of behavior. *"The more arguing the better"*, Satan is thinking. Well, shake him loose. Don't fall into that trap. Don't hash out and go over everything again.

Obviously, the first thing you should do is to not argue. As in the example above, Linda and I simply stopped our conversation and went out to the garage to see what we were both talking about. Linda explained her perception, which I recognized immediately as truth as seen from her prospective. Then I explained my truth from my perspective. Wow, we are both correct as seen from our different perspectives. No argument. We were done and did not have to rehash what each other thought and why we reacted a certain way and on and on.

This is the way to handle these types of situations. Nip it in the bud before it gets out of hand. If you do start down that ugly dark path of argument, you need to stop it whenever you recognize that it is happening. Then go back to the beginning and explain what your line of thinking is to your spouse. Then your spouse should explain what their line of thinking is. Each of you has your own perceptions of what is truth for you. Forget what you each said during the splintered conversations and start completely fresh. You will realize by that point how to explain to your spouse what they had not understood. If you are still having trouble communicating to your mate or understanding them, then drop it and wait until you can verify what is being said. Nothing is that important to argue over. You don't have to be right! It makes no difference to your life if you are right or wrong does it? Don't let your pride get in the way. Most things that people argue over do not matter in the least. In the eternal scheme of things, it doesn't matter if the tool pouch is on the left or on the right, does it? It mattereth not.

Do You Like Your Mate?

Do you like your mate? Do you like what they do? Do you like the way they look? Are there certain aspects that you don't like about them? Are you irritated by how they do things? Who puts these thoughts into your head? As you ask yourself these questions you are probably thinking several things. You are probably thinking, "Of course I like my mate, I love them." Love and like are two different things if you think about it. You can love someone and yet not like the things that they say or do.

Satan is a master at getting us to dislike each other. If he can get us to dislike something about our mate, he knows he can build upon it. It doesn't have to be anything of any degree to lay the foundation of discontent. You as a couple can be totally in love with each other in perfect harmony and yet Satan will whisper to one of you something like, *"Look at the way they comb their hair. Isn't it stupid the way they do that?"* Or he will say to you, *"Isn't that irritating the way they chew their food when they eat?" "They never put their shoes away in the closet. I think they do it just to irritate me."* These are only a fraction of the things that Satan may be whispering to you to get you to dislike something about your mate.

Satan knows that if he can get you to think anything negative about your spouse, he can build on it to make it worse. As with the linking described earlier, he is continually trying to get a foothold in your mind to get you to think something negative about your spouse. If he can, then he will try to link something to that thought and so on. He whispers things into your mind to get you to build a case against your mate. Each one of the things you dislike is chiseling away at the foundation of your love for each other. If you give in to these thoughts and harbor in your heart these dislikes, you are giving into Satan.

Don't give in. When these thoughts come into your mind, get rid of them! If you have already given into many of these thoughts, purge them with the tools you have in this book. Don't let them eat away at you. Picture this. You and your mate are a strong brick wall together. Each time you harbor and agree with Satan's influence about something you dislike about your mate, you are in effect chiseling away at the foundation of your wall. Each time you are taking your hammer and chisel and making a hole in the wall that you and your mate have built together. If you have enough dislikes built up in your mind, you will have chiseled so many holes in the strong wall you built together that it could be starting to shake. If you get enough holes in the wall it could start tumbling down.

What is the solution? Stop focusing on the things you don't like and focus on the things you do like. Talk to your mate about the things that bother you about them. Don't accuse or nag them about it. Discuss it openly and honestly. What can be done about it? Approach it in a loving way to find a solution. Is it that your spouse can change something or do you need to change your perception about the problem? If you approach it in a kind understanding way, I know you can come up with a solution.

If it is something that cannot be changed, like a physical feature, you must change your way of thinking about it. Remember to use the tool, it just is. Accept it for what it is and think no more about it. It will only grow and fester if you think about it. When you put attention on it, it cannot go away. Satan wants you to focus on something that irritates you. He would like nothing more than to keep the things in front of you that cause a negative reaction. Don't put your attention on the irritation. Let it go. It just is. Remember the story I told about Linda and the bug on her windshield. As long as she focused on the bug she was getting more irritated. When she started looking through the rest of the nice clean windshield, she noticed the beauty of the world around her and lost sight of the irritating bug. So focus on the good things about your mate.

Another thing you can do is rehearse several positive things about it in your mind. Think of ways to change the once negative thoughts into positive ones. You should already know how to do this by reading the chapter 4, "I Can't Think Positive, Can I?" Use the tools in this book to help you out of this negative thinking and Satan's influence. Just remember that every little thing that you don't like about your mate can add up to a mountain of little things. One little thing can lead to another. This is yet another way Satan links negative things together.

Here is an example: I had my carpets cleaned by a company that said that they were the best in the area. When they first came out to clean, they did a fantastic job. I couldn't be happier. They next time they cleaned my carpet, I saw that they forgot to clean behind the door in one room. I let it go but it kind of bugged me. The next time they came to clean I mentioned it to them and they took care of it. After they left though, I saw a spot that they didn't quite get as clean as I thought it should be. I thought to myself, "If they didn't get this spot as clean and missed the spot behind the door last time, what else did they miss that I am not aware of?" Then I decided to look around to see what other flaws I could find. Sure enough, I found that they didn't move the dresser out and clean under it. They didn't put protective pads under the legs of some of the furniture. I went looking for reasons to not like this carpet cleaner and I found them. These were minor things that could be corrected if I just let him know about it. The carpet cleaner is human and will make mistakes. Maybe there was a misunderstanding on what was expected. Overall, he did a really good job. If I let this get to me about the little errors, and this is my perception, I just might not call him again to clean my carpets. I would *fire* him.

As you read that story, did you see the analogy I was drawing about disliking things about your spouse? If at first you see something to dislike about your mate, it can cause you to look for other things to dislike, linking one bad thing with another. Each one can build on the other until you have a *case* against your mate. Much like an attorney builds a case using evidence against a felon.

Turn these negative thoughts into positive ones. Discuss the situation and clear it up. Much like as when I called the carpet cleaner and discussed with him what he did. The carpet cleaner was more than happy to come back and clean something he missed and fix what ever other issues I had. I found out that it actually was a misperception on my part as to what he had contracted to do. Once we cleared that up, we were back on good terms. And so it is with your mate. You both should be open to discussing any little irritation between you and clear it up before it links together into a mountain of little irritations. If you work at it, you will see how Satan's suggestions come into your mind.

Once they do, recognize them, remove them and replace them with good thoughts. These three actions will help you to overcome the battle with Satan to influence you to dislike your eternal mate.

Satan Revisiting Something That You Have Worked Through

As you are going through life and using the tools in this book you will find that certain things will creep up and bite you again. What I mean by that is, let's say you have had a certain *moment* where Satan has whispered to you to do or say something. You have overcome the whisperings and thwarted off the dreadful demon and actually had a victory. You might have even had a breakthrough!

This is about something that has been nagging you all your life. A breakthrough is a certain habit or belief about something that you have just suddenly realized was incorrect. You were awakened to the realization that your tightly held belief was an incorrect perception that caused you or someone else grief every time it showed its ugly head. Now you realize that you must change that incorrect perception because you know it's correct and now move ahead in the right direction. You have had an "Aha!" moment, if you will. A huge victory!

So, several days go by after one of these victories and suddenly out of the blue you are attacked by Satan to revisit this old habit or belief. What do you do? Well, first of all, lets back up to the point where you had the victory. After the victory, you need to do a little self examination. What was the belief or action that was incorrect? What is the new belief or action needed to be on track to correct the misperception you previously had? Now take that new belief or action to heart and decide how you will handle it in the future when it comes up again, because it will come up again.

This new belief or action has to take hold in your heart and mind long enough for it to become a habit. Remember, you may have held on to that belief or action for many years so you have to be prepared to overcome the desire to fall back into the old ways. Changing your desire is the first step to regaining freedom from the misperception of the past.

You have to desire to change. Without the desire you might as well be a on a roller coaster in an amusement park just going down the same track day in and day out. You must desire to get off that roller coaster one track thinking and build a new track of your own. Straighten the track if need be, lay it out flat, or make it go higher. You must desire to be great at conquering Satan by bettering yourself and clearing up old misperceptions.

Now that the desire is there, decide upon how you will handle the situation when Satan tempts you again in this area. What will you do? Another tool you can use is a very simple one. As you become aware of the tempting, say something like, "Satan, stop! Go away! I have already worked through this. Satan, I do not believe that anymore." You can say that or you can say whatever you want that fits the situation. Say it out loud whenever possible. Satan cannot hear your thoughts. He needs to be aware that you are not going to give into his whisperings.

I expect myself to say things like the above statement because of the commitment I have made in making positive changes in my life, and you should too. I expect Satan to go away and I will not be seduced into his trap. I expect to have a victory over this temptation. I expect to work through this quickly. I expect that this new thinking or new habit will take hold and bring me more happiness. I expect that this new thinking or new habit will become one of my strengths.

It is better to have high expectations and not reach them than to have low expectations and meet them every time. You will be much more successful and more likely to get better at reaching the high expectations and less likely to be stagnant by always reaching a lower level you are comfortable with. Expect the best and don't get discouraged if you don't live up to your expectations. Even a partial victory is better than no victory at all. Not trying will only bring you defeat.

There are other tools in this book that you could use of course to keep those temptations at bay. You could simply say, "That is not of me, Satan. I will give it no thought or feeling." You could pray to Heavenly Father about it. You could ask him to help you get rid of the thoughts. Ask him to help you overcome these temptations. You could raise your arm to the square and cast Satan out. You could sing a church hymn or listen to one. You could read scriptures to purge that thought from your mind. There are many ways to handle these satanic thoughts and to remove them.

Once you have removed them, fill your mind with positive thoughts. Depending upon the temptation, you could think of the opposite thing that Satan was trying to tempt you with. Filling your mind with scripture, hymns, positive affirmations or positive thoughts about your mate may do the trick. Remember to first recognize these temptations. Then remove them with the tools in this toolbox. Once removed, replace those thoughts with good positive uplifting thoughts.

When Satan whispers to you about something you have already gone through, just get rid of that influence the same way you got rid of it the first time. The reason Satan is revisiting that same area is because you have been weak in that area in the past. He still wants to bring you down and will always hit your weak areas first. The idea is for you to make those weak areas in your life become strengths. Here is how you do it.

> "And if men come unto me I will show unto them their weakness. I give unto men weakness that they may be humble; and my grace is sufficient for all men that humble themselves before me; for if they humble themselves before me, and have faith in me, then will I make weak things become strong unto them." (*Book of Mormon,* Ether 12: 27)

Work on those weaknesses by humbling yourself before God. Have faith that you will overcome those weaknesses and they will become strong unto you. Also, use the tools in this book as well to help you overcome the wiles of the devil and help you progress as a celestial couple quicker.

So, now you have learned how Satan links negative events in your life to make one huge bonfire out of all those little fiery darts. Start to recognize those links so that you can break them. Break that link by actually changing the way you react to it. Tell Satan, "No, I will not give in." You must react differently than you have in the past to a similar situation for there to be a break in the link. Snuff out the fiery darts that cause you to dislike your mate by discussing it with them or by using the 3 R's (Recognize, Remove and Replace). You must keep at it by removing Satan's influence by using the tools in this book. Turn that negative into a positive. Have high expectations that you will come off the conqueror. Humble yourself and have faith that you will overcome your weakness. As you use these tools together with your eternal mate to help you break Satan's negative linking, you will find that not only will you become strong individually but you will become a great strength together.

HELPFUL TOOLS IDENTIFIED OR EXPLAINED IN THIS CHAPTER:

1. Recognize your negative thoughts.
2. Make a promise to Heavenly Father to work on not being offended.
3. Choose to be playful or silly instead of lashing out.
4. You have a choice so choose to react in a positive manner.
5. Laughing.
6. Give no thought or feeling to perceived negative comments or actions.
7. Let it go. Let go of blame or judgment.
8. Don't assume your mate is like you in every way.
9. Clear up any misperceptions your mate has by discussing it openly and lovingly.
10. Discuss with your mate how you will handle this situation in the future.
11. Recognize the pattern and connection of Satan's lies from one situation to another.
12. Recognize the misguided negative thoughts that come into your mind.
13. React positively to all circumstances.
14. Recognize that your mate may have different perceptions than you. They may be looking from a different angle than you.
15. Stop your miscommunications and forget them. Start over from the beginning.
16. Do not rehash the misperceived conversation.

17. You don't have to be right. Don't let your pride get in your way. It mattereth not.
18. Focus on the things you like about your spouse.
19. Discuss openly and honestly in a loving way about the things that bother you about your mate and come up with a solution.
20. It just is. Accept it and think no more about it.
21. Change your negative thoughts into positive ones.
22. Recognize – Remove – Replace.
23. Do a self examination and take the newly corrected belief or action to heart and decide how you will handle it in the future.
24. Desire to change.
25. Say, "Satan stop! Go away! I have already worked through this. Satan, I do not believe that anymore!"
26. Expect the best possible outcome.
27. Pray and ask Heavenly Father for help.
28. Cast Satan out.
29. Sing a church hymn.
30. Read scriptures.
31. Have faith and humble yourself before God.

10

Have You Got The Basics Down Yet?

What are the basics of a strong celestial marriage? You have probably been taught them for years. One of the basics is that you put God first in your life. Everything should be centered on Him. It is by God's law that you will judged. Therefore, it is imperative that you live God's laws and keep His commandments. I am not going to cite a huge list of His commandments to you. You should know what most of them are by now. Put your life in harmony with Him and use the tools here in this book and that will work hand in hand to get you to the Promised Land, the celestial kingdom.

Let's get into what I call the basics. These are all going to be obvious to you once I start naming them off. Now don't roll your eyes just because you have heard about these before. These are essential for the perfect celestial marriage.

1. Couples prayer. I feel that this is something that unifies a couple. A morning and evening prayer together is ideal. I realize that some of you may get up at different times or go to bed at different times. In these cases, you can still have prayer together, just schedule it in somewhere. Of course you should have family prayer as well with the children, but I am only going to concentrate on you as a couple right now.

Sometimes prayer can get lost in the shuffle of kids from here to there as well as within other time consuming events. That is why you should get into a pattern of having prayer together at a certain time every morning and evening. If a certain time doesn't work, pick an event that you can have prayer afterwards. An example of this would be that just as soon as you shut off the TV to go to bed, that's when you have couples prayer. Linda and I have prayer together in the morning just before she leaves to go to work. Pick a time slot and put it in there every day. Be consistent at it until it becomes habit.

Some schedules are hard to get together but you must come up with a solution. At one point in my life I had to get up real early to go to work. I had to leave at 4:00 a.m. to get to work by 5:00 a.m. Linda would get up at 4:50 a.m. and call me on my cell phone just as I would be pulling into the parking space at work. We would have prayer over the phone together before I went into work. That gave her a little extra sleep in the morning. I have also been away on business trips and we have had prayer together over the phone. Whatever the situation is, you should be able to work it out where you have couples prayer.

One thing about prayer that I have found is that if you get out of the habit, it can go by the way side. Both Linda and I are fixed in the habit of having couples prayer in the evening and then we will separate into different rooms where we have designated to say our personal prayers. By working together in this fashion, we have set up a pattern where we do not forget to pray.

I feel that it is super important to thank God for all that we have experienced each day. Be grateful for all that you have. I am so grateful that I am married to the most wonderful woman in the world. Sorry guys, I already have her! Actually, she *is* the most wonderful woman in the world, to me. You should feel the same way about your mate. Be grateful for your health, that you have two arms and legs, that you can walk, talk, see, hear, smell and touch. Be grateful that you are where you are and not someplace worse. Be grateful that you have a roof over your head and food to eat and clothes to wear. Be thankful for your family, friends, and people around you that make life comfortable. Be thankful for the electricity you enjoy that runs all the things you enjoy in your home. Be grateful for the store down the street that stocks food that you can buy and cook on a stove that turns on with a little twist of a button. Do you get my drift here?

Be grateful for all things in your prayers. You don't have to list them all in every prayer, but give thanks for several things that you normally take for granted each time and you will see that it will make a difference on how you look at your life. If you look for things like the water that comes into your house and with a turn of the faucet good clean water comes out. If you are grateful for things like that and look for other small things, you will become aware of how blessed you really are. No matter what station in life you may happen to be in, you can always find something to be grateful for. Don't take anything for granted.

2. Family home evening. This of course is great for the family and creates bonding between kids and parents. Having an evening set aside once a week for the family to get together to learn a gospel principle, spend time with each other, talk about the week, express their concerns, talk about their triumphs, have a fun outing together, etc. will keep your family close together. Since I am writing about couples, I won't write much concerning family home evening except this one thing. If you are a couple without children, set aside this evening for yourselves and make it a habit so that when children do arrive, you have already been in the habit for a while. If you are older and the kids are out of the house, this time is also well spent together. Ok, on to the next basic.

3. Reading scriptures together. This has been a great help to Linda and I. Reading the scriptures has especially opened our eyes to things that we may not have seen when we read it by ourselves. When you read the scriptures together and discuss them as you read, you will find understanding that only couples can have. Each of you sees things differently. Whatever you do, don't just read them for the sake of reading them. Actually discuss them as you read. If something strikes you in the middle of the chapter, stop and talk about it. Maybe you just need to stop and clarify what is going on or what a certain passage means to you. This is where you will learn the most. You will learn the most about your mate. Not just what your mate knows about the scriptures, but what they feel about them and about life as you read together. Yes indeed, you will learn about what the scriptures teach, but you will also learn about each other as long as you talk about what you read.

Find a way to implement what you learn and read about into your daily life. Just as Linda used the scriptures to help her overcome Satan's whisperings by reflecting back on Pahoran and Moroni. She used the, *it mattereth not* scripture we had read together.

Pick a time when you can read the scriptures together. If you have to get up fifteen minutes earlier to get the job done, by all means, get up fifteen minutes earlier! If you have to stay up fifteen minutes later before going to bed, get it done. Read them each and every day together. Never miss! It is so important. Linda and I usually read at least one chapter per day. You can read as little or as much as you like. Whatever you read though, discuss it together.

4. Thoughtful communication. Next, can you think of something that you used to do a lot before you were married? When you were seeing each other before marriage, you would talk on the phone, send love letters, email each other, send text messages, and go on dates. Well, why did you stop? Was it because there was some sort of language in the marriage document that prevented you from all those niceties you used to do when you were single? I don't think so. All of these things are still OK to do now that you are married. In fact, I highly encourage you to continue! Wouldn't it be nice if you guys called home during your work day once in a while to tell your wife that you love and miss her? Wouldn't you guys feel good that your wife sent you a text message saying that you are the love of her life and can't wait until you are home again. What about an email that expressed your heart felt feelings to one another once in a while?

5. Date night. What about going out on a date? A date? I hear you thinking, "Why should we go out on a date, we already got married. Dates are for single people aren't they?" Yes, dates are for single people, and that's what you are going to be if you don't go out on a date with your spouse! Ha ha. That may be a joke, but then again, maybe not. Having a regular date with your spouse may be hard for some of you with small kids and little money for a babysitter I realize. There are ways around this though. I suggest trading off babysitting with another couple that also wants to go out on a date night. You babysit their kids one night and they babysit yours another night. It may only be a few hours, just enough time to get away together to enjoy each other in a different atmosphere. You don't even have to go anywhere expensive. For those of you with kids, if you even planned an event at home when the kids are somewhere else, that might be just as good as going somewhere. There are plenty of places to go and be together without spending a lot of money.

The point here is to do something together where you have interaction and quality time together. Going to the movies together would be nice once in a while, if that is something you enjoy, but I would not advise this every time. Watching a movie together does not give you quality time together. You need interaction time. You need time away from the world, from kids, your job and every other distraction that separates you and your mate. This is together time. Think back to a time when you were dating. What did you do then? I would imagine you focused on each other and blocked the world out, am I right?

One thing you can do on date night is to go to the temple if you are lucky enough to have one near you. This is another basic that needs to be in your life. Go to the temple as often as you can. Go there and feel the spirit that is present there. Get a renewed spirit as you perform ordinances for those who cannot perform them for themselves. I know you will be greatly blessed for attending the temple regularly.

So, those are the basics. You have heard all this before and will need to hear it again. We are all such little children in the gospel. We need to hear the same things over and over again until we get it. Then we need to hear it over again because we started to do what we knew was right but forgot to keep it up. We fall out of the habit.

It is so important to have couples prayer night and morning, hold family home evening, read scriptures together as a couple, enjoy thoughtful communication, have date night and attend the temple together. These things are important to the health of your eternal progression as well as to the health of your eternal marriage. The basics as I call them are the mortar that holds the bricks or building blocks of your celestial marriage together. It is the stuff that fills in the cracks between the blocks that might otherwise fall apart. The building blocks of your celestial marriage, which are the tools in this book, are held together with the mortar from the basics. The mortar surrounds each block and holds it in place so that another building block can be put into place to make you both stronger. As you get your life organized and put the basics into practice you will find that this will help you add building blocks to your marriage as you become a great strength together.

Helpful Tools Identified
Or Explained In This Chapter:

1. Put God first in your life.
2. Set up a time to have couples prayer together as well as personal prayer.
3. Be grateful for all that you have.
4. Read scriptures together and discuss what you have read.
5. Have family home evening.
6. Express your love to your mate through notes, emails, text message, a phone call from work, etc.
7. Go on dates with your mate once a week.
8. Go to the temple as often as possible.

11

ARE YOU 100 PERCENT COMMITTED?

Commitment is a huge word and hurdle for a lot of people. Commitment in this world seems to mean that you will stick with something until it becomes hard and then look for something else that is easier. Isn't that what you see in the world today? It is so easy to get married and so easy to get divorced. In a couples mind these days they are thinking, "I love the person I am marrying (if they get married at all), but if they become too hard to live with or for some reason it doesn't work out, we'll get a divorce and I'll find someone else." The grass will be greener then, right? Commitment is a big part of a couple's up front feelings before marriage but is lost sometimes after marriage.

Let me first tell you a little story about the love affair a lot of us have with our cars. First you love having the new car and driving it around. You take care of it and treat it nice and you feel good about it. You wash it and keep it nice and clean. You get the oil changed on it regularly and give it the maintenance it deserves. After all, you plan on keeping this car a long time. Then you get your first dent in it. Oh darn! Now it is not new any more. Then the stereo knob breaks off because you were a little rough with it. The kids spill red fruit punch on the back seat and floor. You get a few more scratches here and there and now the car isn't looking as good as it did. You start neglecting the car little by little because of all the flaws that are on it now. You stop washing it and changing the oil as often as you should. After a few years the car is looking pretty sad and you are tired of it. The car starts to have a little mechanical trouble because you have neglected the maintenance. Your car is not running as good as it used to, so you start looking at other cars and wishing you had a newer, better one. This gets you thinking along the lines that you don't really want this car anymore. You would like to get a different model. You want a new car that you could start all over with again. You know you would be happier if you just had a newer model. This time, when you get the newer model, you promise yourself that you will keep it up better than the last car. You will treat it better and wash it more often and maintain it better so it won't break down.

Now, as you read through the above story, what were you thinking? Were you putting your spouse in the place of the car? In many households around the country, spouses are treating their mates just like a car, aren't they? Well, you are the only one that can say if you are or not. Your spouse is not an object to be discarded like an old car when you are done with them. Just because you have mechanical breakdowns sometimes with your mate doesn't give you a reason to trade them off! A car is an earthly possession that will definitely wear out. An eternal marriage is something that will not wear out. That's why they call it an *eternal* marriage. An eternity is a long time. You must deal with what you have in this short life to prove you are king and queen material because you have a long way to go after this.

Make a commitment now to your mate that will be everlasting. If you get a few dings and scratches along the way, patch them up and buff them out and get on with your commitment. Sometimes you may get into an accident, or something that will cause a lot more stress in your lives. Maybe some major event puts your marriage in jeopardy and is difficult to overcome. If you have been working on your marriage as you go along, you will be able to work through such a catastrophe. Just as you must to have car insurance, you must have marriage insurance.

The insurance of which I speak is this. You must be 100 percent committed to one another. You must believe in as well as believe one another. Be honest with one another and use positive reinforcement to help each other through good and bad times. These and other tools have been created for you to use to insure that you will not only survive as a celestial couple but will prosper in love and harmony. The tools in this book are your best insurance if and when a catastrophe hits.

I find that most couples forget their original commitment to each other. They really don't work on their marriage like they would if it were a business. It is one of the most serious business' you will ever contract to do. It not only impacts you while you are in mortality, but will affect how your eternity will end up. Do you want a happy eternity or an empty one? I will be talking to you in a minute about how we can remind ourselves about this commitment so that you never forget.

Making a commitment is not a foreign thing for you. We make several of them starting with baptism and moving on to temple covenants. As we go to the temple and participate there, we are reminded of the covenants we made. This is great to do if you live in an area where you can go at least once a month. In Sacrament meetings we are reminded about the promises we made at baptism and renew those covenants by partaking of the sacrament.

So how do you get reminded about your marriage commitment if you only go to the temple once a month or less? This is what I suggest. Linda and I use affirmations to reaffirm our commitment to one another. This is only one of many ways to be reminded. Each morning whether it is while you are in the shower, doing a workout, driving to work or to school, or whenever you choose, say something like this several times with feeling: "I am 100 percent committed to my mate. My mate is 100 percent committed to me. I will always speak in a soft loving tone to my mate. My mate loves me and I want to be a good husband/wife to him/her. I will recognize Satan's whisperings and stop them before they cause trouble. I am 100 percent committed to my mate."

Of course I want you to fill in your mates name anywhere it says "my mate." You can use these words or make up your own. The point here is that I want you to remind yourself that you are 100 percent committed to doing what it takes to make your marriage a marriage that will last an eternity.

If you say this affirmation with conviction and emotion, it will become so engrained in you that you won't have to think about it. It even works better if you will visualize something that had a real positive impact on you that your spouse did or said while you are saying the affirmations with conviction. It will sink in subconsciously to where it will become a part of your core self. This is what you are seeking after. If you are 100 percent committed to your eternal mate, you will be unshaken if you get hit broadside with some tragedy or hardship that would normally drive couples of the world apart. Make the commitment to each other. Remind yourselves of this commitment each day and let your partner know that you appreciate their commitment to you. This will help you stay focused on each other. A great thing will happen if you do this. I promise you that if you are 100 percent committed to each other nothing will get in your way.

Where do I put these affirmations so that I can remember to say them? One suggestion would be to write them down on a 3X5 card and put that card some place where you will see it often. You may put that card in your scriptures as a marker so you will see it when you read as a couple. Linda and I have typed them up and put them in a sheet protector and have hung them on the wall in the bathroom. You may type them into your PDA or cell phone with a daily reminder. Search for a way to remind your self to read those affirmations every day.

Does Your Wife Or Husband Matter To You?

Be sensitive to your spouse. Make them feel that they matter. Sometimes, life happens and we get so engrossed in something that we make our spouse feel that they don't matter to us. Stop and make sure that your spouse feels that they matter to you. It may be in a certain area that they feel that way. It is up to the spouse that is feeling that they don't matter to bring it up to the other spouse in a loving way.

Say something like, "Honey, when you make decisions about so and so with your parents (or what ever the problem is that it makes you feel you don't matter), I feel like my input doesn't matter to you. I would like to know that what I do, say or feel matters to you. Please help me to understand." Then discuss this between you. This should not be an attack on the other spouse but simply a desire to understand how and why this is happening. There may be a very simple explanation such as the other spouse just didn't realize what he or she was doing. It could have been an old habit or tradition that needs to be adjusted.

What ever the reason, there is no need to get into an attacking mode or a defensive posture. This simply needs to be talked out and aim for a solution. The idea is to come up with a solution that will make the both of you feel that you matter to each other.

Here is an example: George and Martha are empty nesters and take care of Martha's father Jerome who lives with them. Martha has a sister Debbie who lives on the other side of town but rarely comes to see her father Jerome. Jerome was complaining that he would like to see Debbie more often. One day, Martha was talking to Debbie and mentioned this to her. They both decided that Debbie should come over once a week to visit and Martha would cook dinner.

This worked out very well. On the night of the visits, the four of them, George, Martha, Jerome and Debbie would play board games during the visit. Each time they would play various games. The games were mostly decided by Jerome, Martha or Debbie. Each time George would make a suggestion no one paid attention.

After several months, George finally talked to Martha. He felt that he didn't matter to Martha. He felt that every time he wanted to do something on that night, he was ignored. He also was not even consulted when the one night a week visit by Debbie was set up. George just felt that it didn't matter what he said or did.

After hearing what George told Martha, she began to think. This is the way we have always done it. When she and her sister got together, since they have always been close, they would always make decisions together concerning their parents. It was a habit that they just did. Martha wasn't aware that she was doing anything wrong. Through the discussion between George and Martha, she could see where she was slighting her husband. She was not giving him an opportunity to be heard. She was not making him feel that he was more important than her sister or father.

Sometimes this is a quick fix and sometimes more work may need to be done to resolve this. Both of you need to be open and considerate of each others feelings. Never dispute the other spouse's feelings. You may not agree on certain tangible items or thoughts and ideas, but you should never tell your spouse that you don't agree with their feelings.

You may not like what your husband or wife is feeling, but just the same, they are feeling it. The words that you say may help them feel differently but never, never say something like, "How could you feel that way?" Never say, "You can't feel that way." or "You shouldn't feel that way." They do feel that way and the only way to help them feel another way is to talk about it and resolve the feeling. Then provide a new action to prove that the old feeling has been resolved. The new action itself will reinforce the new positive action for a positive result.

What on earth does that mean you are wondering? Ok, here's how you do it. Find out what it is that makes them feel the way they do. Then figure out how to resolve the reasons for the feelings. Usually this will require some action from the spouse that has made the other spouse feel bad.

Let's take the example above. After George explained about not feeling important to Martha, the two of them talked about it. Martha came to the realization that she was in the wrong. She realized that this was a habit that she and her sister have had for a long time. She discovered that George did not feel that he mattered to Martha because she had not consulted George in this matter. Also, she did not listen to Georges request on any activities to be done on that night. Realizing this, Martha told George that she would include him from now on. She also asked George if it was ok to continue with this weekly event, to which George agreed. This made George feel better for the time being. Now it is up to Martha to follow through with the action that would prove her intent. Over the next few weeks, Martha would ask George what he would like to do on those nights. Sometimes George had a suggestion and sometimes not. George really felt that Martha cared about him and saw that he mattered to Martha.

Use this formula to make sure that you matter to one another. You should put your spouse first in your life and make sure that they know that. Make sure that you are 100 percent committed to your eternal mate. Say affirmations daily to reaffirm your commitment. By doing this and thinking about one another your bond will get tighter and tighter. By keeping in mind that you are 100 percent committed to making a wonderful eternal marriage and putting your spouse first, you are creating a bond that will make you a great strength together.

HELPFUL TOOLS IDENTIFIED
OR EXPLAINED IN THIS CHAPTER:

1. Make sure you are 100 percent committed to your mate.
2. Believe in your mate.
3. Believe your mate.
4. Be honest with your mate.
5. Use positive reinforcement with your mate.
6. Go to the temple together.
7. Use affirmations with conviction and emotion.
8. Recognize Satan's whisperings.
9. Discuss how each of you show how you matter to the other.
10. Be open and considerate of each others feelings as you resolve issues.

12
DISCUSS THESE THINGS TOGETHER.

One of the best tools in this book is the art of discussing your fears, anxieties, trials, weaknesses, temptations, complaints, etc with your eternal companion. After each day or at minimum every couple days get together and discuss everyday challenges, defeats, and victories. Let each other know what you are working on and how you dealt with it during the day. Tell what the situation was and how you overcame it and what tools you used to help you. If you didn't use any tools and the temptation seemed to engulf you, discuss how you could have done better and what tools to use next time this happens.

This is very helpful because most of us need a sounding board and an objective view to look at our situation. If we are going to help one another, we need to know what challenges our companions are facing. A lot of the time it will involve us anyway. We can help our companion and visa versa especially when it comes to being positive or negative. When we are in a negative mode, it is hard to spot by our self. By talking about the issues of the day, we can spot some of the negativity in what our spouse is experiencing and thus help them to correct it.

I know that this will seem strange and foreign to most women. It is well known that most women just want to be heard and understood as they talk to their husbands. They generally don't want the husband to come up with solutions to *fix* the problem. Well, we are not fixing problems here. We are making life changes so that *problems* don't occur. Oh yeah? I can hear you now, "Do you honestly think we can make life changes so that we don't have any problems?" No, that's not what I am saying. What I am saying is that if we can fix ourselves it will alleviate most of the problems we face in life.

If you see that a water faucet has old and rusted pipes going to it and you ignore it, you are ignoring a possible problem. If you ignore it long enough, the pipe may burst and cause flooding throughout the house. This would cause more damage than was necessary if you had only fixed the pipe in the first place. Such is the case when I am talking about you *fixing* yourself before the possible eruption.

Talking with your spouse is an excellent way for you to check up on the rusty pipe so to speak and to keep an eye on it while you are fixing it. Talking helps your spouse recognize what needs fixing, helps to remove the negative thoughts and actions and then helps to replace the negativity with good thoughts and actions.

I think we as mortals tend to be rather complacent by not putting any effort into our growth. We need to be asking ourselves often, "How can I improve myself and get better at winning this battle against Satan?" By talking with our spouse on a regular basis we are able to tune up our skills as observers and problem solvers. We need these skills in order to find out how Satan is attacking us and where we need to build up our defenses. Don't make light of this battle. It is a war indeed and we need to be focused on winning each battle so that in the end, we will be victorious.

WHAT TRIGGERS YOU?

As you talk together as a couple, seek to recognize thought patterns and behavior patterns. Satan has a way of attacking your weakest areas and he will do it consistently and methodically. If he can, he will get you to think that there is no use in fighting against him. He will try to wear you down. By talking to your spouse about these patterns it will help you to understand what is going on. The two of you can work on a solution together. There may be certain *triggers* that make you respond a certain way. A trigger is something that when it happens, it causes you to react in a certain way. An example would be that someone tells you that you are fat. That might stir up an emotion in you that would cause you to lash out at someone and start calling them names or you may hit the other person. The statement that you are fat is a negative trigger.

Find out what those negative triggers are and see if you can remove them. Here are a couple of examples of removing negative triggers.

I worked at this one job for a while and the guys that worked with me liked to cuss and swear like sailors. I would cringe every time I had to listen to this kind of language. The trigger, the bad language, would irritate and agitate me. One day I had too much of this language and I decided to ask them not to speak that way around me while we were working together. Amazingly, they complied. I had thus removed the negative trigger.

The other type of trigger is action oriented. Let's say the husband is sitting there watching TV with clicker in hand. The wife knows that he should be doing something else, like mow the lawn and take out the trash. The longer he sits there and watches TV, the more the wife gets upset. If the wife asks the husband in a nice and calm way if he would please do these things and the husband gets up and does them, the trigger that was making the wife upset is removed. On the other hand, if the wife is sarcastic in her approach to the husband or yells at him, this will create a negative trigger in the husband. He may just sit there out of spite and continue to watch TV. This does no one any good. A discussion later about this by the couple can help resolve any further triggered response by the wife if they come to an appropriate solution that will satisfy both of them. Between a husband and wife, all negative triggers should be resolved. Remember, you are working together as a celestial couple.

If you can't remove the negative trigger, think of a tool or tools that will help you through the temptation that influences you react negatively. The first thing you need to do of course is to recognize the trigger. What is it exactly that triggers your feeling to react the way you do? The object here is to train your self to feel differently when that trigger happens again. The idea is to disrupt the pattern so that the original trigger won't work the same way it has in the past. Then to set in place a new trigger that will turn a negative behavior into a positive result.

Here is an example: I told this story earlier in chapter 2 and is worth repeating to illustrate how to turn a trigger into a positive result. It was where Linda and I were reading together one evening when the phone rang. After I took the phone call I got distracted with a couple other things before I got back to Linda. I thought Linda was waiting for me patiently but she wasn't. Inside she was getting impatient, frustrated and rather upset that I was doing all these other things while she was just sitting there waiting for me. Satan was throwing negative thoughts into her mind to do something that would have disrupted the whole rest of our evening. Fortunately, she used a couple of tools to counteract Satan's attempt to split us up. First she used the, *this is not of me* tool to recognize that the whisperings were not of her but from Satan. Then she used the *prayer* tool for help. Once I got back to reading with her, she was able to completely calm down.

Since Linda was able to recognize this trigger, me taking so long and making her wait, she had refused to believe that this whispering was from her. Then she used the *prayer* tool to help her pop it out of her mind. Since that time, there have been times that she has turned this trigger into a happy moment.

Here is an example: As we are getting ready for bed, there are times that I am a little later in getting into bed than Linda. So picture this, we are both in bed with the lights out. I suddenly remember that I haven't turned the heat down for the night so I get up and adjust the heat. I come back to bed and then realize that I forgot to take my vitamins, so I get up and do that. I get back to bed and then I realize that I need to set the alarm. At this time, Linda is being disturbed by me and she would like to get some sleep at some point, right? Normally she would start to be annoyed at this point. So I set my alarm and get back to into bed. Then I think of one more thing and I say, "Shoot." Linda hears me and she says to me, "Are you going to make a phone call, clip your nails, and clean off the stove?" Then she laughs and that makes me laugh. At that point, she has turned the trigger of waiting on me to a positive reaction. She has brought this up to me several times since as she is triggered by me and each time we laugh about it.

What we are accomplishing here is to take a situation and change the way we feel about it and turn it into a positive reaction. Remember, it's not what happens to us that cause the negative reaction, it is what we feel about what happens to us that causes the reaction. If we can change the way we feel about a certain thing when it happens then we will be able to change the reaction. Don't be a victim by thinking you can't change your feelings toward what happens to you, because you can. Once you have the desire and decide to change your feelings about what happens to you, you will be taking control of your life. Taking control of your life is a beautiful thing when you can turn a negative around to a positive.

Some situations may not be as easy as this to change the negative feelings into positive ones. Let's say that you are on the highway and as you are driving along, someone cuts you off or pulls in front of you or doesn't give you the right of way when you are clearly in the right. Everyone who has been driving for any length of time has run across an incident where you were irritated by someone else's lack of driving skills. Sorry to say that most drivers who have been irritated by this kind of behavior seldom think of anything nice to say about the other driver. This is a trigger for most of us, right? Of course it is. As you read this you are probably thinking of an incident that recently happened to you, right? I know you can relate. So, how can we take this negative trigger that hits us square in the face and turn it into a positive?

Let's get out *How To Build Marriage Unity That Will Endure Throughout All Eternity* and see what we can come up with. Ahhhh, first of all, you must not take it personally. They would have done that maneuver in front of anyone. They didn't just single you out. They probably don't even know you. They might not even be aware of their bad driving behavior. They might not even know better because no one ever pointed out to them that they were doing anything wrong. Now that you don't take it personally, you can't be offended can you? Offended is a deeper step that a lot of us jump to right off the bat. So don't take it personally so you won't be offended.

Have charity in your heart. If you have charity in your heart, you won't judge or categorize someone else. You would give them the benefit of the doubt and accept someone's weaknesses, shortcomings and differences and have patience with them.

So, what if they did cut you off? Do you think yelling and screaming at them from inside your car will correct their bad behavior? I am sure that they won't even hear you. Yes you can hand signal them to let them know you are angry with them but what does that accomplish? You may not ever see that person again to know if the hand signal you gave them has changed their behavior or not. Besides, you can't change them by this little encounter. You need to change you. You are the only one that has control over how you feel. Let's go on.

You need to accept what just happened without blame or judgment. Accept and give thanks that no one got into an accident and no one was hurt.

I do feel you need to express your verbal concern for the individual that cut you off though. Yes, you need to express it whether they can hear you or not. I want you to say, "Bless you," as they do what they do. Then you need to forgive them and let it go. Release it in your mind and think no more about it. By using several tools in this book you can accomplish a peacefulness that you may have never felt before about situations like these.

Thinking of all these things I have just mentioned can take about one or two seconds of time but can relieve a day's worth of frustration. You know what I mean. You are on your way to work and something like what I was describing happens to you. You get so upset about this incident that you think about it through the day. This negative thought pattern draws to you other negative things that happen to you throughout your day. You start to think, "My day started off bad from the beginning and now my whole day has been bad. This always happens to me," and yes, it does. You will need to have the desire to change your current behavior. Change that negative reaction into a positive one and you will attract positive things. Continue to work on the various triggers that wear on you and make you feel negative. Think of ways to turn it around to a positive.

So, what does this last bit of information have to do with discussing things together? It must first start with you. You must recognize these triggers and discuss them with your spouse. Eliminate these harmful triggers between the both of you. Honor each other by fixing what you can so that those triggers are removed.

As you are working on removing triggers between yourselves, act as a coach for one another to help with other triggers that pop up in life. No, I don't mean nag each other about situations that they don't quite have under control yet. I mean soft gentle reminders to help each other when they are not doing as well as they could in certain circumstances to get them on track again. One of the best statements that go along with most circumstances is, "Dear, how could you say that differently?" Or you could say, "How could you rephrase that?" Anytime I hear statements like these from my wife I immediately see that she hears negativity coming from my mouth. I will stop and think of a new statement that will turn what I just said into a positive one. Then I will say it in a positive manner.

As you work together and talk about these types of challenges you and your spouse will work out agreements between you on how you will handle certain situations. Just as when either Linda or I say a negative statement, the other will give the gentle reminder with a smile on their face, "Dear, how could you say that differently?" We have set this up ahead of time and we both agreed that it would be a trigger to make us stop and assess what we have just said and say it in a positive manner. This works very effectively to eliminate the common irritation of hounding or nagging. Since we have agreed and both of us use it from time to time, it has actually been a very positive tool. It is almost like a game. If I have unknowingly just made a negative comment and Linda recognizes it and gives me the gentle reminder, I smile and realize that she is only trying to help me along the path of eternal perfection.

As you discuss these triggers together and are open and honest about what is really happening in your life, you will discover a strength that was never there before. Some of these frustrations you have may be able to be solved by the two of you discussing them and trying to find a positive solution. Remember, you are working on the solution on how you feel about a situation and not about the situation itself. There are of course many situations that will never be resolved to your satisfaction so the only way to deal with it is to change the way you feel about it. Work with what you can. Work on you.

Your spouse can only give you suggestions and can't do it for you. Once you have come up with a solution, implement it and continue to use it. Discuss your progress with your spouse as situations confront you. If after you use this strategy for a while and it doesn't seem to work, discuss it again and work something else out. I know you will come up with the right solution as you work together.

TURNING NEGATIVE TRIGGERS INTO STRENGTHS

1. Recognize the trigger.
2. Remove the trigger if possible or replace it with a positive trigger.
3. Do not take it personally.
4. Do not be offended.
5. Do not judge the other person or situation. It happened and it just is.
6. Develop unconditional love. You may dislike what someone does but don't hate them, love them. Say, "Bless you." instead of cursing them or the situation.
7. Release the negative emotion attached to the event.
8. Forgive them and let it go. Don't dwell on it. It happened, so what, get on with your life and think no more about it. Once you truly forgive, and let it go, you will feel a peace that you have done the right thing.

Talk these things over with your eternal mate and be sincere in taking control of your life. Help each other to speak in a positive manner. Turn negative situations into positive ones and if needed, give gentle reminders. Set things up ahead of time what you will say in certain situations to help get your mate back on track. The two of you should work together to eliminate triggered responses between you and others by removing the trigger or changing your feelings concerning it. After removing the negative feeling and response to the trigger, replace it with a new positive one (bless you). Forgive and forget. As you both work on these things you will find a huge difference in the quality of your life. You will have a peaceful feeling come upon you that you have never felt before. You both need to work on these things individually and together. As you discuss this chapter remember, you can only do so much as individuals, but as eternal mates, you are a great strength together.

Helpful Tools Identified
Or Explained In This Chapter:

1. Discuss your fears, anxieties, trials, weaknesses, temptations, complaints, challenges and victories with your mate.
2. Help your spouse to see the negativity your spouse is experiencing.
3. Recognize what needs fixing in your mate and help them remove negative thoughts and actions.
4. Help your mate replace those negative thoughts and actions with good positive ones.
5. Recognize thought and behavior patterns in your mate.
6. Work on solutions together.
7. Recognize what your negative triggers are.
8. Remove a negative trigger if possible.
9. Train yourself to react differently when negative triggers appear.
10. Recognize the trigger, disrupt the trigger and replace with a new positive response.
11. Recognize the negative whisperings from Satan.
12. Change the way you feel about the trigger into a positive reaction.
13. *This is not of me* tool. Do not believe Satan's whisperings.
14. Turn the negative trigger into a funny trigger.
15. Desire and decide to change how you feel about the negative trigger.
16. Don't take it personally.
17. Don't be offended.
18. Have charity in your heart.
19. Don't judge.
20. Accept someone's weaknesses, shortcomings and differences.
21. Have patience with others.
22. Accept what happens without blame or judgment.
23. Give thanks.
24. Say, "Bless you."
25. Forgive.
26. Let it go.
27. Release it in your mind.

28. Change the negative reaction into a positive one.
29. Act as a coach for your mate as they act as a coach for you.
30. Use soft gentle reminders.
31. *How could you say that differently* or *how could you rephrase that?*
32. Work out agreements ahead of time how you and your mate will handle certain situations.
33. Once you have come up with a solution, continue to use it as long as it works for the two of you.
34. Discuss your progress with your spouse.
35. Adjust your plan as necessary.
36. *It just is* tool.
37. Develop unconditional love for each other.
38. Release negative emotion attached to the negative event.
39. Work on using the tools in this book individually and together.

13
Huh, I Have A Love Language?

One of the most misperceptions that couples have is how to love their partner in the way that they like to be loved. Husbands especially are subject to being clueless when the wife just expects him to know everything about her. "Well if he loves me, he should know how I like to be loved." she says. In most cases, nothing could be further from the truth. I will have to admit that most men are not the most sensitive creatures in the world. On the other hand, a lot of women just think that a man has only one thing on his mind, right? This is not always the case. This chapter alone could be one of the most valuable pieces of information that you will ever receive regarding your relationship and how to love your partner. Let's explore some of the ways that we humans like to be loved.

I stumbled across a very enlightening book called, *The Five Love Languages,* by Gary Chapman. The following commentary that I shall write is strongly based on this book. It has transformed my life and opened my eyes to how I can love my partner and how they can love me. It takes most of the guesswork out of what your spouse expects from you in order for them to feel loved.

Typically, here is the way most relationships love each other. Let's say that Bill feels really loved by his spouse Betty when she fixes Bill a hamburger. Bill eats the hamburger and is filled with love. Let's say that Betty feels most loved by Bill when he fixes her a green salad. One day, Bill feels down and he wants some love from Betty. So Betty goes into the kitchen and fixes a green salad for Bill. After all, that's the way she likes to be loved. She gives it to Bill and he says, "Honey, that's nice but I want more love." So Betty goes back into the kitchen and makes an even bigger green salad and brings it to Bill. Bill groans and takes a few bites but then says to Betty, "I thought you were going to love me. All I want is for you to love me. Can't you give me some love?" So Betty goes out into the back yard and gathers up all the fresh veggies from the garden. She washes them and puts them into three huge bowls. She has fixed the biggest nicest green salads you have ever seen and brings them into Bill. Now Bill is so frustrated he just stomps out of the house leaving Betty sad and dismayed. Betty doesn't know what happened. She loved him with as much love as she had. She couldn't have given any more. Betty did not realize that Bills love language was hamburger and not green salad.

That is the way I think most couples live there lives. Not knowing how to love their mate in the way that they like to be loved. When I first started thinking about how I like to be loved, it was hard for me to pinpoint how I actually like to be loved. I thought one way and then another. It wasn't until I discovered that there were five basic ways that people want to be loved that I zeroed in on my primary and secondary love language. I will describe these love languages one by one in no particular order.

WORDS OF AFFIRMATION

Words of affirmation is the first one I will describe. This love language is probably one of the most sorely missed positive events in our lives. As I look at modern couples today as they communicate with their sharp criticism and cut downs of one another, it makes me wonder why they got married in the first place. Remember when you were dating? You were nice and complimentary. You were thankful and appreciative of each other. You hung on every word the other said so you could find commonality and agreement as you looked for the things that you felt the same way about. After couples get married it seems that reality hits them in the face. They suddenly find out that the one they married isn't so perfect after all. Then they start to look for ways to *improve* the other spouse and start criticizing them. This becomes a habit until they are nitpicking them to death.

Couples with good relationships will always use words of affirmation to bring positive feedback into their lives. People love to be appreciated and by saying positive things about what they are doing or saying is showing that appreciation. This can be a primary love language for some people. It can be a motivator to them to do what they do. For example, if a wife is always *hounding* her husband to take out the trash and his primary love language is words of affirmation, this will not motivate him to action. What the wife needs to realize is that hounding her husband is very negative. Her husband wants to hear positive comments of how good he is doing. This will motivate him to do better. Positive words of affirmation statements should go like this: "Honey, I sure appreciate you taking out the trash. You are so helpful to me when you take out the trash. Thank you so much." Don't say statements like, "It's about time you took out the trash," to a words of affirmation primary love language person. This is not what motivates them. They seek positive statements to affirm that what they do is good, helpful, kind, valuable, appreciated, etc. The words you use when talking to them are important.

If your spouse has words of affirmation as their primary love language, make sure you appreciate even the smallest and mundane things that they do by telling them so. It may be that they pay the bills on time, keep a clean house, take the kids to school every day, wash the car each week, earn a living, put their dirty clothes in the laundry, mows the lawn each week, buys groceries, washes clothes and puts them away each week, etc. Use words of affirmation especially when the task is something that is *expected* as part of the duties in life. Thank the other person and praise them by affirming how great they do the particular task. Watch how really good they get at it when they know they are appreciated and hear you as you verbally show the appreciation.

QUALITY TIME

Quality time is where the two of you have time together to talk and to pay attention to one another. It is to be with each other without distraction. It could be that you are at an activity the both of you enjoy together that requires interaction with each other. No, sitting in front of the TV together does not qualify as quality time. Sitting together and reading a book, each taking turns reading, is spending quality time together. Linda and I love to read together and discuss the books we read. We are continuing to learn more and more about each other as we read about different subjects and discuss them.

Always read positive uplifting books. I believe that reading together can bring two people closer together faster than almost anything else. This gives you things to talk about. Not only things about the book, but different experiences you have had will come to light as you read. This gives you an opportunity to share those experiences and discuss them. It might even bring back memories that you shared together.

Riding bikes around the neighborhood, a picnic in the park, go for a walk, learn a language together, go dancing, write a book together, give each other a massage, go to a museum, ice or roller skating, play a board game, and do a hobby together are all good ways to spend quality time together. You get the idea don't you? You can make up your own list. Anything that you like to do together where your intent is to enjoy spending time with one another is making the person who loves quality time feel loved.

RECEIVING GIFTS

A person who has receiving gifts as their primary love language usually perceives the gift as a symbol of another person's love for them. It is a visual and tangible sign that someone has thought about them and loves them enough to give them a gift. It is proof to them that they have been thought about by the person giving the gift.

One might think that this could be an expensive proposition if your spouse always wants gifts from you to show your love to them. It could be, but consider this. If money is your concern, giving gifts to him or her might very well be the best investment you could ever make. You are investing in your relationship. You are fulfilling your mate's needs to be loved. If you show your spouse the love that he or she needs, it is more likely that they will give love to you in the way that you need to feel loved. When you are both getting the love you need in your own appointed way, your bond will grow tighter and tighter. Your joy will be full.

Giving gifts does not always have to cost a lot. Most times it is not the gift itself that is of great worth but it is the though behind the gift. A couple of suggestions might be to buy a card that that expresses your love to them. An even less expensive way to express your love is fold up a piece of paper in the shape of a card and write something of your own to express your love. You could write I love you or something you appreciate about your mate on a little piece of paper and hide it some place where they will find it as they go throughout their day. I have found that if you sat down and wrote a few paragraphs to your mate about how you feel about them or what you admire about them or show your appreciation for what they do and give it to them, they will really feel loved by you.

ACTS OF SERVICE

Service is one area that every one of us gives. Every one of us does something for someone else at least one time in our life. In reality, most of us give service every day of our lives to someone else, but when acts of service is one's primary love language, it is in the forefront of that persons mind. They are likely to give more service than anyone else and thus they expect it from others. They can easily be irritated when others sit around and don't offer to do anything while they are doing all the work. In fact, people tend to criticize others where their most emotional needs are not being met. Thus, if someone is telling you to get up and get busy doing something and they are consistent in doing so, this might be a clue that acts of service could be their primary or secondary love language. They are looking for love and by your act of service whether it be taking out the trash, feeding the baby, washing the car, cooking dinner, washing the dishes or whatever, you are providing the love they seek.

Picture this. Sue is in the kitchen after dinner cleaning up the dishes and wiping off the table. Pete is sitting in the living room with the clicker watching TV. As Sue is cleaning up the mess in the kitchen, she is getting madder and madder that Pete is just sitting there doing nothing while she is doing all the work. Sue's primary love language is acts of service. Suddenly, Pete comes into the kitchen and starts to wash the dishes. He says, "I am sorry dear, I just wanted to catch the news a little bit to see who won the game today. Why don't you sit and relax while I finish up?" Sue, after being shocked that Pete came back to help her said, "OK, I'll go see what the kids are up to." As Sue goes off to find the kids she thinks, "Pete really loves me. He is willing to help me."

Many times with acts of service it may be small things that you can do for someone that brings them constant joy and the feeling of being loved. It is amazing what will happen when a husband will come home and change the babies diaper or perform some other act of service for his wife. How good it would feel to a husband when a wife keeps a clean house because that is important to him. Little acts of service go a long way in showing your love to a person whose love language is acts of service.

On the other hand, if nothing is being done for them, it could be as if you were stabbing them in the heart. If the spouse whose love language is acts of service sees that the other spouse is lazy or does things only for themselves, it makes them feel so unloved. As this happens there grows resentment and anger toward the non servicing partner.

How do you recognize if you or your spouse has acts of service as their primary love language? Generally, spouses who criticize their mate more often in the area of service or lack thereof, tend to give more service and crave service as their love language. Their criticism is their way of asking for their spouse to love them in the way they like to be loved. Recognizing acts of service in a spouse that is *nagging* all the time could really be a blessing. You now know how to fix it and love that person in the way they like to be loved.

Physical Touch

We all know that physical touch is very important. Babies long for the touch of their mother. Little children love to be hugged by their parents and feel secure when doing so. As we become adults, sometimes we lose that yearning for touch as we did when we were little, and yet, many still feel loved when they are touched.

Let's define what I mean by physical touch. This could include a friendly embrace, a kiss, a pat on the back, a touch by the hand on the face, holding hands, a pat on the knee, rubbing legs under the table, all the way to full out love making. Anything where you are making physical contact with your spouse makes you feel loved. To a person whose love language is physical touch, closeness is imperative. It is the primary way that they communicate their love. It is a quick barometer of how they feel in the relationship. The more closeness, the more love they feel.

Now you are probably wondering if physical touch is a love language, then this must be the love language of most men, right? You may think because most men like to get their wives in bed that this would be their love language, right? This is just not so. Men are wired different and have urges brought on by physical reactions in their bodies. This is not to be confused by feeling love when he is holding hands with his wife. Feeling loved when there is physical contact is emotionally based. Yes the contact is *physical* but it makes them *feel* loved. So, if a man does not enjoy other types of touching in a non sexual way, this may not be his primary love language.

People with physical touch as their primary love language enjoy their spouse touching them in many different ways. The deliberate touching sends a signal loud and clear that *I love you*. The touch is heard more loud and clear as *love*, than words could ever convey. A person will feel loved especially when the touching comes at a time when it might not be a touching moment, such as a hug hello or goodbye. You could touch your legs together under the table as you have dinner. When in the presence of friends hold hands or put your arm around their waist or on their shoulder as you talk. Give them a massage or a foot rub. You can think of more ways than this I am sure. Let your imagination run wild.

Many men take this physical touch thing as a sign that their wife wants to head for the bedroom. Please take this advice guys, all that touching, kissing and hugging does not always have to end up in the bedroom. If your wife has physical touch as her primary love language, she is just expressing her love to you in the way that she likes to be loved. It doesn't always have to end up in the bedroom. Be respectful of what she is actually expressing to you. What I am attempting to do here is to have you both discover your primary and secondary love languages so that you both can love each other the way that you both want.

How Do I Know What My Love Language Is?

After you have read through the five love languages as I have briefly described them, you may have already decided which one is your primary and which is your secondary love language. You may have already discovered what your spouse's love languages are. For those of you that are struggling to know for sure, let me tell you how to do this.

Take a look at the history of your marriage. Dig out the archives and put them on the table. "Ahhhhhhh," you say, "now what?" OK, now this is what you ask yourself, "What have I wanted from my spouse the most that they were not doing or giving me? What has my spouse done for me that made me feel loved and closer to them? In what way do I show love to my spouse?" These are questions that should give you a clue as to what your love language is. Write down the answers on a piece of paper. Look them over and see where they fit into one of the five categories. Think of as many things as you can to write down on that list. You will begin to see a pattern emerge and there will be your answer.

If you are still having trouble discovering your love language, either you are very happy and content with the way things are going or you are on the opposite end of the scale and have not been loved in any way for so long you forgot what it was like to be loved. At any rate, I suggest that you pick up the book *The Five Love Languages* by Gary Chapman and read it. It will describe in much more detail what I have briefly summed up in this chapter. Gary Chapman has done a fine job in explaining the love languages and even has a test in the back of the book to pinpoint your exact love languages in their order from first to the last.

This may very well be the most important information you have learned when it comes to loving your eternal companion. Read it over and over and find ways to incorporate it into your lives and you will develop a bond that will carry you throughout the eternities. Each of us want to be loved in our own language or we will not feel as close to our eternal mate as we could. The goal of this chapter is to help you and your eternal mate to recognize how to love each other so that the two of you will have that ultimate bond with one another as you become a great strength together.

Helpful Tools Identified Or Explained In This Chapter:

1. Love your mate in the language they need to be loved.
2. Words of affirmation.
3. Compliment your mate.
4. Be thankful towards your mate.
5. Appreciate your mate.
6. Quality time.
7. Talking and paying attention to one another.
8. Reading positive uplifting books together and discussing them.
9. Enjoying favorite activities together.
10. Giving and receiving gifts.
11. Acts of service.
12. Physical touch.
13. Write down the answers to the questions under the, "How do I know what my love language is?" sub heading.
14. Buy and read *The Five Love Languages* by Gary Chapman. Take the test in the book to pinpoint your love language.

14

COMMONALITIES ARE A PLUS!

One of the things that brought you two together is that you had things in common with each other. As you were dating, you would find things about the other person that were the same as you. You liked that this new found friend liked the same things you did, or you found out that you liked the same things they did. You had common ground. The two of you belong to the same church, like to roller skate, ride bikes, loved to read together, enjoyed the same type of humor, and like the same kind of music are just some examples of commonalities.

There are also many ways to have commonality in an uncommon way as well. I knew a couple where he liked to fish but she didn't. She just liked to be around him so she could talk to him. They didn't particularly like the same thing but they could each accomplish what they wanted as he sat and fished at the lake while she was able to have her talk time with him.

At first when people get married, it seems to be easy to do some of the things that couples did when they were dating. This of course is depending upon the circumstances. But generally, as time goes on and life gets in the way, I believe that couples need to reassess what there commonalities are. The idea is to get back to basics. What are your interests now?

Each of you should take out a sheet of paper and write down your current interests, hobbies, sports, activities, church callings, things you like to do that are fun to you, and whatever comes to your mind. Also make a list of things that you would like to do that you have never done. List goals, ambitions, dreams, places you want to visit, and things you want to accomplish. Let your mind be open and write down everything with no limitation. Each of you should be writing a separate list. After you are both done, compare your lists. Look for commonalities. You may be surprised at some of the things on your spouse's list. Discuss how you might accomplish these things together.

Has your list changed since you have been married? How can these new interests enhance your marriage? In what way can the two of you get together in these new interests that will help you stay close together? Are the old interests still valid? What are you doing together and what are you doing separately? Are these interests pulling you apart or helping you stay close together? What interests should you seriously discard from your life and which shall you cultivate? What dreams and aspirations do the two of you have in common? How can you help your spouse realize their dream?

These are just some of the questions you should be asking yourselves. One interest that should be on the top of every couples list should be that they want to be a celestial couple and to make it to the celestial kingdom together. This should be your number one goal in this life. In reality, there is no other activity in this world that you could do that would bring you as great a joy in the hereafter than to be worthy of the celestial kingdom and to be a celestial couple. This should be your primary goal. This is one huge commonality that the two of you should be focused on. You both need to be on the same page. Are you?

If your current interests and activities are separating you, then you need to take a second look at how they are affecting you and your celestial mate. Is it really necessary that this activity take place? Is your desire to fulfill your pleasure in this thing greater than your desire for a celestial marriage? If you choose wrongly you could be looking back after this life is over and asking yourself, "Why did I do all that *fun* stuff instead of concentrating on my celestial marriage? Why did I spend so much time watching TV?"

> "For behold, this life is the time for men to prepare to meet God; yea, behold the day of this life is the day for men to perform their labors." (*Book of Mormon,* Alma 34: 32).

My point is that we need to examine what is a good and what is not a good interest or activity to pursue when comparing it to our celestial marriage. We are only here on this earth for a short time in comparison to the eternities. Let's make the best of our time. Once you are in the celestial kingdom with your mate, you can have as much fun as you like. Let's get there first.

Oh Yeah, Let's Have Some Fun

There should also be some fun things that a couple can enjoy together. You need to have laughter and happy times in your life to carry you through the sad times. Include some fun activities that you have in common. Look at your lists. Pick out some things that you both enjoy doing together. Also look at integrating activities such as the example of the man fishing and the woman wanting to talk. There are so many variables on this topic that I cannot list them all. Talk about it and come up with a plan so that you can spend time together.

I mentioned laughter earlier. This is an activity I feel that is lacking in a lot of marriages. Life gets to be so serious for most people and some even forget to laugh. Laughter cures the ills that one faces in life. Look at little children. They love to laugh and have fun. You were a child once, remember? You liked to laugh and carry on I am sure. But as we become adults, somehow we lose that sense of fun and silliness and start to become boring. Some of us think it's not too dignified or something and begin to be more serious. These types of people get embarrassed when something silly happens and refuse to laugh in case someone sees them. Lighten up! Be silly! Who cares! Enjoy life!

You need to cultivate the ability to laugh at yourself. Some people will get mad at themselves or others when something happens to them unexpectedly. My wife Linda is the queen of silly sometimes. We were at a fast food restaurant one day and she inadvertently knocked over her milkshake while she was eating. She said, "Oh, look at that." She picked up the cup and then knocked it over again. She picked it up again and then tossed it in the air and caught it. "See what I can do?" I looked at her and immediately knocked over my cup and picked it up and tossed it in the air and caught it. I said, "Yeah, I can do that too!" We both laughed at our silliness. She was presented an opportunity to laugh at herself and went beyond. She turned a potential embarrassing moment into a laughing moment.

Laughter is free for the taking. One does not have to go anywhere or do anything special to receive it. One only needs to look at the things around to see the humor. You can find humor by looking at yourself. If you learn to laugh at yourself, you will be much happier, along with those around you.

Look for opportunities to laugh with your spouse. Don't be so grownup-ish! Be a little silly sometimes. No, it is not dignified, but it sure is fun. I will take fun over dignified anytime. This is not to say you should not be dignified in some situations, but overall you need to not take life so seriously. More illnesses are caused by stressed out serious people who do not know how to laugh. Laughing is the best medicine, even when you are not sick. I believe it can prevent certain illnesses from setting in. You know, it is real hard to be depressed when you are laughing don't you think?

"A merry heart doeth good like a medicine." (*Bible*, King James Version, Proverbs 17: 22)

Another side of laughter is that it drives evil spirits away. Do you think Satan is going to stick around while you are having fun and laughing with your spouse? I believe laughter is a shield that can protect you from Satan's fiery darts. He cannot penetrate through the laughter. His dark whisperings cannot enter your mind. The opposite of laughter is sadness right? Satan likes you to feel sadness and despair. When you are feeling happy with laughter, you are on the Lord's side of the line and are more under His influence.

Laughter has a power of its own. It has the ability to strengthen relationships and bond people together. Laughter can diffuse tension and win hearts. It has the ability to mend broken hearts, repair relationships and bring good feelings back that were once lost.

Studies on laughter have been shown to heal the body to a certain extent, help people live longer happier lives, be more creative and productive, give people more energy and have less physical discomfort. Blood pressure decreases, heart rate decreases, the body releases endorphins and depression is reduced with humor. Humor dispels anger, resentment, fear, stress, and embarrassment. It definitely heals the mind and spirit.

So, you and your mate get out your pens and paper and start writing down your current interests, hobbies, sports activities, church callings, things that you like to do that are fun to you and whatever else comes to your mind. Compare these lists and see where you have commonalities. Plan some things that you can do together. Decide what you should keep on your list and what you should discard. Keep in mind that your goal here is to be an eternal couple and some activities may not be in keeping with this goal. Some activities may be separating you too much so you may want to re-evaluate whether or not you should continue with this activity. Temporary *fun* is not worth losing your eternal companion over. Seek for activities you can enjoy together.

Now that you know more about laughter and humor and why you should have more of it, start laughing today! Don't be a stuffed shirt or a stick in the mud. As it gets into evening before going to bed ask your spouse, "Have we laughed enough today?" If not, do something silly like make faces at each other or think of something you did that was silly today and tell your spouse. You should know each other well enough to find something to laugh about. A family that laughs together stays together. As you find things in common to do together and to laugh about with each other, you will find that your anxieties will melt away because your laughter helps you to be a great strength together.

HELPFUL TOOLS IDENTIFIED
OR EXPLAINED IN THIS CHAPTER:

1. Reassess your commonalities.
2. You and your mate make separate lists of your interests, hobbies,

sports activities, church callings, things that you like to do that are fun to you and whatever else comes to your mind. Discuss how you can integrate the two together.

3. You and your mate make separate lists of things you would like to do that you have never done and compare lists. Discuss how you might accomplish these things together.

4. List your goals, ambitions, dreams etc. and discuss them with your mate. Start by asking questions that are in this chapter.

5. Come up with a plan so that you are making the best of your time together to enhance your progression as a celestial couple.

6. Laughter.

7. Laugh at yourself.

15
ARE YOU OPEN OR CLOSED?

Are you feeling open or closed? Everyone has feelings. Whether you choose to show your feelings or not is up to you. You can hide them from someone and keep them to yourself. You may suppress them to save you hurt from what you have to deal with in life. You may wear your feelings on your sleeve and let everyone know how you feel. You may express your feelings openly all the time or only share them when you feel they need to be expressed. You may bottle your feelings up inside keeping them to yourself so at the right moment you can release them like an explosion upon some unwilling participant. Feelings can be handled so many different ways and these are just a few examples.

What are feelings? One dictionary defines one aspect of feelings as: an emotion or emotional perception or attitude: *a feeling of joy; a feeling of sorrow.* It is something within you. It is your perception of what is happening to you or around you. This perception forms an attitude that you carry with you. It is a measuring stick with which you measure subsequent events. With this measuring stick, you compare the new data you receive today with what has happened in the past. As you measure it and compare it, your heart swells within you and creates emotion. After the emotion is created about what just happened, your brain computes all this data. It includes the surrounding situation both physical and emotional. It brings in what was said and done along with the smell, taste, touch, sight and sound. Your brain is taking in all this data and trying to make a decision. All this may only take a millisecond.

Events that happen in your life may quickly stab you in the heart or make you feel happy and joyful. It could bring a feeling of love or hate. Feelings come very quickly and decisively and can strike you to the core. Feelings can get you into trouble. Feelings can get you out of trouble. As in life, there are good feelings and bad feelings. Good and evil if you will.

Do you always listen to your feelings? Do you know what they are actually telling you? Do you get mixed feelings? Are you confused by your feelings? Are you overwhelmed by your feelings sometimes? Do you wonder why you are feeling a certain way when you really don't want to feel that way? What is going on with my feelings anyway?

Entire books have been written about feelings. I won't be able to cover everything that you should know about feelings here, but will concentrate on a few aspects of feelings, why they are important and how you should use these feelings to your advantage. I don't mean to take advantage of another person because they are feeling a certain way. I mean that by understanding your feelings and managing them properly, they will become an advantage to you in your life. The advantage is that you will become closer to your Heavenly Father and to your eternal mate.

Are you open with your feelings or are you closed up, not wanting others to know how you feel? I find that people who are open with what they are feeling are more loving, kind and sincere about wanting to work on relationships to make them better. People who are *closed down* with their feelings tend to think negatively, have more anger built up inside and are not as willing to talk about or improve their relationship with their spouse. These are two extreme examples and of course, there are many different degrees of openness between the two.

What are you feeling right now after you just read the previous paragraph? Chances are that you identified with one of the two extreme examples. You either said, "He is right on." or you said, "This guy doesn't know a mountain from a mole hill." right? Well, if you think I am wrong, just keep reading and see if I know what I am talking about.

I find that most people in general are closed minded when it comes to new things. If something doesn't meet the normal standards of what they have known all their life, they discount it or totally don't believe it. They say, "That can't be so." or "I have never seen or heard anything about that before so I don't believe you." If you look at all the things we have in the world today you will see some fantastic advances. If you told someone one hundred years ago that you could talk to someone in another country with a little hand held device, they would have laughed at you and considered sending you to the insane asylum. Don't you agree? Yet that is what we are able to do with today's cell phone. One hundred years ago this technology was available if someone had invented it. All the elements were there one hundred years ago to do what we are doing today. It was as possible then as it is today.

Now, the person that would have laughed at you one hundred years ago was closed minded wasn't he? Yes, I agree that it was not possible at that time because no one had invented it yet, but aside from that, it was possible just as it is today. It took someone with an open mind to say, "Hey, I think that I can invent a portable telephone that people can call anyone in the world and talk to them on their way to work." Someone with an open mind and a goal to see what others with a closed mind could not see.

How closed minded are you to things that are out in the world? When new ideas that you have never heard about are presented to you, do you say, "I don't believe that garbage!" Do you say instead, "Hmmm, that looks interesting. I didn't know that existed and I would like to find out more about it so I can see if it will benefit me or my family." Some people are so closed minded about things that they close themselves off from something that could ultimately benefit them. Once they hear about a product, for example, that someone else tells them about, even though what that person said was incorrect, they already assume that they know enough about the product and are not open to learn more about it to see if it will benefit them.

Let me give you an example: Ellen is seventy two years old and owns a home in a nice neighborhood. Her husband passed away a few months ago. This has left her a little tight on income since she would not be receiving any more of her husband's pension or Social Security money. She owns her home but has a small mortgage on it with a payment of $500 per month. Ellen's only income is from Social Security which is $1,365 per month. Ellen saw an ad on TV about a reverse mortgage and talked to Nancy about it. Nancy had heard that years ago people were losing their home to banks using a reverse mortgage. Nancy told Ellen that they were bad and that she might as well sell her home rather than give it to the bank. At that point, that was all that Ellen needed to hear and she closed her mind to anyone who would try to point out to her how it would benefit her.

After a couple of years, Ellen was not able to keep up with her expenses and was getting deeper and deeper in debt. She couldn't afford to pay the minimum payments on her credit cards and the house was getting in disrepair. She could not stay afloat financially. In her despair, she finally was open to almost anything that would help. She talked to a professional about a reverse mortgage. She found out that the bank doesn't own the house. She owns the house just like she does now. She found out that a reverse mortgage would have helped her all along for the past few years so she wouldn't have had to struggle like she did. She found out a lot of things that her friend Nancy didn't know about that was positive and good about the reverse mortgage. Ellen found out that by using the reverse mortgage, there was a way that she would never run out of money if she used it wisely. Since she did not have to make house payments, she would save that $500 per month in her pocket that she had been paying her previous lender. This gave her more income.

Ok, so what's the point? The point is, that if Ellen had been open minded enough to investigate what a reverse mortgage was all about instead of being closed minded after what Nancy had said, she could have avoided years of struggle. The point is to never be closed to new ideas no matter what other people say about it. Don't just take one persons word for something and not investigate it further. Be open to new ideas, products and services. If you are not open, you are closing off a possible opportunity in your life. I am not saying that everything that is presented to you, you must purchase or try out. I am saying at least investigate or look into what is being presented to find out if it is good for you. Be open minded and you will be surprised at how many opportunities will come your way.

Open Up Your Feelings

Think about how open minded you are. At least you are open minded enough to read this book! That is fantastic! How open minded are you to learning and applying what you are reading? OK, now that I have talked about being open minded, let's talk about being open with your feelings.

Opening up your feelings is so important when talking with your spouse. When you open up and divulge your most inner thoughts and feelings to your spouse, you can become connected in a way that will bring you much joy and inner peace. When you communicate your feelings, there is a oneness that occurs. I am talking about feelings of love, charity, gratitude, and forgiveness. These are divine characteristics that cause you and your mate to be one with each other.

Heavenly Father has given us feelings for many reasons. One way He communicates with us is through our feelings. Just as Satan whispers to us to cause negative feelings, our Heavenly Father uses the Holy Ghost to whisper positive things to us which gives us positive feelings. Are you open to these feelings or promptings from the Holy Ghost? The more you are open with your feelings, the more you will feel the presence of the Holy Ghost. If you shut down your feelings and hide them you will find it hard to feel promptings of the spirit. If you are suppressing your feelings you are suppressing the spirit. You are hardening your heart. Who are you hardening your heart against?

I can't express to you how important it is to be open to feeling the Holy Ghost when it prompts you. You cannot have a closed heart and receive promptings from the spirit. This is not a door that you can open and shut as you please. You must work on opening up your feelings to your mate on a continuous basis in order to stay in tune with the spirit.

Some men think that they have to so be strong in front of their woman that they don't show any sort of emotion, like shedding of tears. They have to be macho and manly. This is the world's view of men. Eliminate this from your mind. Shedding tears does not show weakness in a man. It shows compassion and meekness. Meekness is not weakness. It shows strength and self control.

A man does not benefit by being Mr. Macho. This may be strength in the eyes of the world, but to a woman, you are a rock. When your wife is being emotional and she comes to you for comfort, and you show no emotion, she may as well go lay down on the bed and water her pillow. She wants you to be emotionally connected with her. She wants you to show your emotions to her.

Guys, don't be afraid to show your positive emotion. Let your guard down. It's ok to cry in front of your eternal mate. It's ok to show your tender emotion. Women love to see that their husbands care. They want their husbands to show their emotional side. Wives feel connected with their husbands when they do this. It's time that you husbands feel connected to your wives. You know the kind of feelings I am talking about don't you? I am talking about feelings of love, appreciation, patience, compassion, understanding and acceptance. I am not talking about those feelings on the opposite side of the scale that breeds disconnectedness and disharmony.

I don't mean to put this all on the husbands because there are many women that have shut down their feelings as well. There are many reasons that someone would be shut down emotionally. I believe that some people have not been taught by their parents how to show their emotions or the parents have just not allowed them to express their emotions adequately. Others have had such traumatic things happen to them that as a defense from further hurt, they choose not to display and actually suppress their emotions. People who have a hard time showing or dealing with their own emotions and feelings have a hard time in a relationship.

Work on opening up your emotions with your spouse. You will find a world of good things at your fingertips. Don't be afraid of getting hurt if you open up. You are not weak or wimpy if you show your emotions. If you are embarrassed about it because the *world* has told you to be, let that feeling go. Learn to trust your eternal mate. At the same time, don't trample your eternal mate's feelings when they are expressed to you. Never laugh at your mate or ridicule them when the open up to you. When your mate expresses their feelings to you, don't deny them or tell them that they shouldn't feel that way. They do feel that way whether they want to or not. Listen to them and fully experience what their feelings are and see what your feelings have to offer.

So, be open to the fact that you don't know everything and when you only know part of something don't assume you have enough information to make a decision. Be open to the fact that there are other things in this universe that may seem strange to you now but maybe fifty years from now these strange things will become commonplace. Be open to new ideas that stretch your thinking.

Remember that one way Heavenly Father communicates to us is through our feelings. We feel His influence through promptings from the Holy Ghost. If your feelings are shut down, you may not be able to feel those positive promptings of the spirit.

Open up your emotional side and tell your feelings to your mate. Let these feelings flow openly and honestly. See how these feelings will bring you and your eternal companion closer together as you become more connected. As you work on expressing your deep positive feelings about one another and really open up, you will find that you will have great strength together.

HELPFUL TOOLS IDENTIFIED
OR EXPLAINED IN THIS CHAPTER:

1. Be open-minded and don't assume anything. Search for the facts.
2. Open up your feelings to your spouse.
3. Show your positive emotion to your mate.
4. Listen to your spouse when they express their feelings to you.
5. Trust your eternal mate.

16
RECOGNIZE EACH OTHERS
ATTITUDE AND DEMEANOR.

You may already know your spouses true attitude and demeanor by living with them so long. You may not know these features about your spouse at all. You may think you know but until you use the tools in this book, you may just be guessing. By using these tools, the both of you will get down to your core self, your true beliefs and attitudes about things. You need to recognize your spouse's outward attitude and demeanor in order to help them.

What do I mean by this? We are put here on earth to be tried and tested. We have our free agency. We are enticed by good and evil. I believe that our true self is happy and we want to be with God and taste of His goodness. When we are at peace with nothing negative flowing within our bodies and are happy and optimistic about life, this is our true self. Think about how your spouse looks when they are happy and at peace. This is what you want to remember when you are with them. This is how you always want them to be, right? Keep that picture in your mind.

When Satan is whispering to your spouse and they are giving in, you need to spot it right away and help them to stop it. You are a team! Act like a team and help each other. Satan is there wanting to split you up. It is your job to help each other become victorious in this second estate. By noticing your spouse's attitude and demeanor, you can nip the argument in the bud before it gets started. Let me tell you a story of what happened to me.

Linda and I decided to get pizza for the family home evening dinner one night. We had invited my brother over to enjoy the evening with us. Linda is very selective about what she will eat. She is very health conscious and eats mostly vegetables and very little meat. Just a couple times a year she will break down and eat some pizza.

As Linda and I are deciding what to order she says, "I want to suggest something, no, I want to put in my order. I want a personal pan pizza with the things I want on it." I said, "OK." and I called my brother to see what he wanted on the pizza. He wasn't home so I left a message for him. The message I left was, "Hey Bro, we are having pizza tonight and wanted to know what you wanted on it and whether you liked thick or thin crust. Let me know as soon as you can. Thanks."

Linda heard me and complimented me on how nice I was for asking him what he wanted. I responded by saying, "Well, it's only courteous." "That's great of you." Linda said. "Why do you think that's so great of me, I am just being considerate." I snapped back with attitude. Linda looked at me and put up her hand, palm toward me and said, "Stop stop stop!" I stopped. She told me that I was looking *dark* and had a negative attitude. She noticed that my demeanor had changed and I wasn't looking like my normal self.

After a few seconds I recognized that she was right. I smiled at her and said, "Thank you for saving me." in a sweet and tender way as we hugged. Satan had whispered to me to get offended and snap back at Linda. This has been a weakness in the past for me and Satan knew it. In the past I have always had a hard time accepting compliments. Linda helped me to recognize that Satan had influenced me and that I was following his lead. She recognized it because of the change in me. She said I looked dark. My demeanor had changed and a countenance of darkness had come over me. Learn to recognize this in your spouse and help them to get rid of it. Let's continue with the moment.

We then started to talk about how if my brother calls back and wants thick crust and I don't care what kind of crust, that we could order one large pizza. Linda started to get a little bit insistent about that she wanted her little pan pizza her way and what if my brother wanted thin crust and we could do whatever we want and blah blah blah. She was going on and on about it with a bunch of attitude like I was earlier. I could tell her attitude was going south.

There are certain things about Linda that really stand out to me when Satan is influencing her. She starts talking faster and doesn't let me get a word in edgewise. Her face changes to a real sour look and she has a lot of *I am right and you are wrong* attitude in her voice. All these signs are so unlike her. Normally she is a very happy positive person with a smile on her face and a lot of patience. To me, it is the difference between night and day.

So, as she was talking, I put my hand up, palm toward her and said, "Stop stop stop." She immediately stopped and said, "Oh!" and started to laugh. "Oh my gosh, Satan just tried to get both of us." We both started laughing. We both helped each other to recognize what was happening and that allowed us to adjust our attitude and put smiles on our faces once again. To finish the story, we ordered the pizza after my brother called. We got one large pizza that satisfied us all.

By understanding your spouses true self, attitude and outward appearance, you can head off a possible confrontation. When using the "Stop stop stop" tool, you must set this up ahead of time, that you will recognize it when your spouse uses it to help you. Never use the stop stop stop tool in any other way. If you do, it will not be effective when you need it to stop the satanic whisperings to your spouse when you really need it. Never use it to stop an already ensuing argument just so you can get control of the conversation to do more battle. You must use it only to help your companion recognize Satan's influence so they can counteract that influence. When you say "Stop stop stop," it must be in a normal tone of voice. Never yell or scream it.

Seek to recognize your companion's inner and outer appearance. Is the face you are looking at the true person or has Satan whispered things to them that is influencing them to look different? Notice the attitude change from the pleasing to the harsh. Sometimes you may think that these thoughts or actions are coming from the person themselves and that Satan hasn't got anything to do with how the person is acting. Through my researching, testing, living and trying new concepts and ideas found within these pages, I have found that Satan is at the root of almost 100 percent of all the negative experiences we have.

How Do I Know If It's Me Or Satan?

Once you get to know your spouse and the good positive things that come from them, you will know them. The good that is in every person *is* them. The bad or negative things are of Satan. We are all basically good people and yet we allow Satan to influence us to do his work by spreading negativity, evil and destruction to our fellow man. Some people think that these feelings and ambitions are just who they are. This is one of Satan's lies and deceptions. He has been influencing us since childhood. He has been at us for so long that we believe the negative feelings we have are just who we are. Nothing could be further from the truth.

Do you like who you are? I hope you do. There may be some aspects of yourself that you don't like though. What is it that you don't like about yourself? Chances are, Satan has influenced you to think do or say that which you don't like about yourself. It could be that you get angry quickly, are lazy, are impatient, are quick to judge others and then find out that you were wrong about them, or some other irritating thing you don't like about yourself. Satan has influenced you so long that you think there could be no turning back and no erasing those negative traits that are engrained in your system. How do I know this? Let's see what the scriptures say.

> ".., for there is nothing which is good save it comes from the Lord: and that which is evil cometh from the devil." (*Book of Mormon,* Omni 1: 25)

> "And behold, others he flattereth away, and telleth them there is no hell; and he saith unto them: I am no devil, for there is none—and thus he whispereth in their ears, until he grasps them with his awful chains,

from whence there is no deliverance." (*Book of Mormon*, 2 Nephi 28: 22)

Satan, the devil, not only whispereth that there is no devil, but everything he can think of to influence you to do evil. How do I know this for sure? How do I know that he is influencing you to do evil? How do I know that it is not just your personality to take advantage of another or to steal or lie or be mean to some one? There is a simple test, you know. There are a couple of things you can do to find out.

You must recognize at the time what you are feeling when you have done something negative or when a negative thought comes into your mind. The easiest way is when you are having a discussion about something and you feel argumentative. Stop and think about how you are feeling. Are you agitated? Is your heart racing a hundred miles an hour? Is your breathing rate faster? Does your heart feel like it will explode because it is so tight in your chest? Then think about what you have said. Are the things you are saying negative or positive? Notice all these things about yourself. It will take less than five seconds. Then go to step two.

This is a simple yet powerful tool. I suggest that after you have taken full account of what you are thinking and feeling that you cast Satan out. This is a simple procedure and takes less than five seconds. Anyone can do it by raising your arm to the square and saying something like "Satan, I command you to leave us and this home now, in the name of Jesus Christ." You do this in the name of Jesus Christ and by His power. You must have faith in Jesus Christ and believe that Satan will indeed be cast out. This is essential. Once you have done so, take a big deep breath and see how that makes you feel. More than likely you will feel better or *lighter*. You may have felt the spirit tell you, Satan is gone. Many people feel this in various ways. Stop and think about it. Do you feel a relief? More than likely you will feel different than when you were agitated earlier. Notice you are calmer than before. Notice that you aren't thinking those negative thoughts and are not as combative as you were. Yes, you may still disagree with whom ever you were conversing with before, but it will take on a new spirit. Satan wants to put pressure on you and influence you to argue. He has trained you for a long time and you are just responding the way you have always done in the past. So much so that you think it has always been you that were argumentative. Try this a few times having faith that you have cast Satan out and you will be amazed at how much better you feel.

Another method is to stop and have a silent prayer if you are around other people, or pray aloud if you are by yourself. This method works very well and can be used in combination with method one. Everyone has their own style of praying but I will suggest something that you may or may not have thought about. In praying for relief from Satan's influence, you might want to keep this in mind. While praying to your Father in Heaven, tell Him what happened. As in the example from above, tell Him that some negative thoughts came into your mind and you said them to whom you were conversing. Tell Him that you didn't recognize those thoughts were from Satan and how you feel about what just happened. Ask Him to help you recognize Satan's whisperings sooner so that you can stop them in your mind and not say them. Ask Him for forgiveness for saying and thinking those thoughts. Ask Him to clear those negative thoughts and feelings from your cells, from your DNA, and from your whole body. Ask for strength mentally, physically, spiritually, and emotionally to overcome Satan's temptings. Add anything else that you think is appropriate.

By doing one or both of these methods of getting rid of Satan, you will find peace. You will find that there are two sides to you. There is the real you, and there is the you that is influenced by Satan. You may or may not be able to recognized the real you versus the you that is under the influence of Satan.

HELP YOUR MATE RECOGNIZE SATAN'S INFLUENCE

Since I know that you are working on this with your beloved eternal mate, be observant of how your mate changes when they are under the influence. You should be able to recognize it in them before they will recognize it themselves, at least at first. Watch each other closely. When you see your spouse is under Satan's influence, stop them. Help them to recognize what they are doing or saying.

When I say stop them, I don't mean that you should hit them over the head with a frying pan or something. You should set this up ahead of time. Set up a signal that you both agree on that when this signal is enacted, the person under the influence will immediately stop and assess their behavior. (Linda and I had done this in the example above when we were ordering pizza.) They need to look at what they are doing and cast Satan out or pray about the situation or whatever works for them so that they can get rid of Satan's influence. No conversation should continue until you are no longer under Satan's influence. Your relationship with your spouse is so much more important than continuing to go down the path you were headed. The first step is to recognize Satan's influence. Then you must remove it and then replace it with good positive thoughts.

Remember, anything from God is positive and anything negative is from Satan. Test and try the tools here in *How To Build Marriage Unity That Will Endure Throughout All Eternity* and see if they don't make a huge impact on your lives. You will be surprised at how much influence Satan has over us when you are not using these tools. Once you cast him out a few times with the use of these tools, you will be as convinced as I am he has more influence in our daily lives than you think. You have more power than him and can remove his presence thus limiting the influence he has over you.

Don't Take It Personally

I know I have discussed this before in a previous chapter but I think at this point you need a little reminder. In recognizing your mate's demeanor as it changes while they are saying mean things to you, you have got to remember not to take it personally. They are under the influence of Satan. You have got to separate them from what they say. In other words, recognize that what they say is not of them. Satan is influencing them to say stuff to you that will make you angry and want to fight back. If you take it personally that's exactly what will happen. You will fight back.

Your objective at this point should be to open your eternal mate's eyes to see what is happening to them. Sometimes it is right before their eyes but they can't see it. Your job is to help them to see what they are doing.

I had an experience with this recently. Linda and I were driving along trying to find a certain address. I had printed out an online map to help us get there. Unfortunately this was a new area and the map I printed out was not showing all the roads that were really there. The map wasn't working for me. I remembered that I had a handheld GPS system with me. I plugged in the address where I wanted to go and it started to give me the directions and turns I should take. Linda was curious about how the GPS worked and decided to take a look at it.

Linda picked up the GPS and stared at it. She moved it around from side to side. She raised it up in the air and looked. She said, "I can't see it." I looked at her and said, "Take off your sunglasses. You might be able to see it better." As she took off her sunglasses she looked at me and smiled and said, "Thanks for uncovering my eyes!" We laughed and Linda said, "You should put that in your book as an experience where one mate is uncovering the others eyes."

I wish life was as simple as taking off a pair of sunglasses. Your objective is to help your mate see what they cannot see or are unwilling to see right at that moment. Use the tools that you have already learned about to accomplish this. Here are nine steps that you can use to help your mate see their actions more clearly when they are saying things to you that could be considered offensive:

1. **Don't take it personally.** Remember it is Satan behind what they are saying.
2. **Disassociate your spouse from what they are being influenced to say**. Anything you would say to your spouse in a negative way in rebuttal to what Satan wants them to say is going to hurt them. If you separate the two, Satan and your spouse, you will be less likely to say anything back to them that would hurt them. Please note that while your mate is under the influence of Satan, anything negative you say will be heard by your spouse and Satan will help them to feel you are attacking them personally. Satan wants you to attack back at him by yelling at your spouse. Does that make sense?
3. **You must stay in control and don't become offended.** No matter what happens or what is said, if you don't take it personally you shouldn't become offended. You have got to

remember that what is said by your spouse is not of him or her but of the satanic influence.

4. **You must speak in a soft loving tone of voice while discussing what is going on.** Do not confront what is being said by your eternal mate until you have calmed them down and have gotten rid of Satan's influence. *This is key!* You cannot reason with Satan. He is not reasonable. Every lie, half truth, excuse, dirty trick, blame, accusation etc. will come forth if you don't get rid of his influence quickly.

5. **You must get rid of that influence by using one or more of the tools in this book.** You can cast him out, have a prayer, sing a church hymn, read some scriptures or whatever you can do to rid yourselves of his influence. Once you have recognized that he is gone, you can then resume the conversation continuing in soft and loving tones.

6. **You must discuss and clear up any negative act or situation with each other that started the whole thing in the first place.** Make sure you are continuing to speak in soft loving tones of understanding. If your speaking tones get elevated and angry again, go back to step five.

7. **Discuss the situation and come up with a solution.** Once you have a solution and have resolved the situation totally, you should discuss what happened, how to avoid it in the future, and what you will do if it happens again (what steps you will take to get your spouse out of that situation should it happen again).

8. **You must ask for forgiveness from your mate.** Do it in the right way. Don't just say you are sorry. Ask your mate to forgive you. The forgiving mate should forgive quickly by saying, "I forgive you." If both of you have done something that needs forgiving, make sure you both go through this procedure. Then you are ready for the last step.

9. **You should have a victory song or dance or whatever lifts your hearts together.** Rejoice over the victory over Satan and your ability to have power over him. Rejoice at the victory and have love in your hearts for each other. You have helped one another and should be grateful to the helping spouse that

uncovered the eyes of the other. This is where you are a great strength together. Always help each other to *see clearly* what needs to be done to bring harmony back into your lives. I promise if you do this, you will have a happiness that you have never felt before.

Awww, C'mon Coach!

Have you ever had a coach? I am not just talking about sports here. A coach could be someone that helps you to succeed at something. They are a teacher and a cheerleader. They can also be a motivator and a goal setter for achievement. A coach might help us to be a great piano player, basketball star, singer, runner, a great speaker, a politician, a writer, almost anything.

In my opinion, coaching is one of the most powerful forces on the planet. When there is a true bond between the coach and the player (I will use player as the term for the one being coached), there isn't anything that the two of them can't do together. Coaching is all about faith in the player. The coach has faith that if the player does what he coaches him to do he will be successful to reach the goal that they have set together. In most cases, the coach has faith in the player to go beyond what the player thinks he can do. This is evident in the fact that the player needs the coach to encourage him along to get better. The coach can see the potential of the player in his mind. He can see as the player performs what he has been capable of doing in the past and can visualize what is needed for the player to reach his full potential in the future. The coach looks for ways to improve the player and sets forth a new plan when needed. As there is improvement, the coach adjusts and sets a new game plan to reach the desired results. The coach is always observing and looking for new and better ways to perfect his player.

On the other hand, the player must have complete faith in the coach. The player knows the coach is right and knows what he is doing. When the coach tells the player to do this or that, the player responds by doing just what is asked. Sometimes the coach is suggesting something that is foreign or hard to accomplish at first. The player tries diligently to complete the task as best he can. After much practice the player is now performing the task beautifully. Sometimes the task that the coach has explained to the player looks to be impossible to perform. What is it that brings the player to the point that helps them go beyond what they think they can do? It is the faith in the coach that the player has that makes him try this new thing that looks impossible. They do it because the coach has worked so hard with them. They do it because they don't want to let the coach down. They stretch themselves beyond what they even imagined they could do because of the faith in the coach. They have the faith that the coach will be there by their side to help them.

This is why the player accomplishes more than they could if they didn't have a coach. The coach sees in them a higher potential than they see in themselves. The coach pushes them on to achieve and accomplish what they could not do for themselves. I believe that each of us is that way. We do not see our own potential. We stop before we hit the mark. We need someone to help us get to and exceed the mark. That's where our eternal mate comes into play. Each of us needs to coach each other. We need to coach each other in the way suggested above. If we are focused on our eternal mate and are coaching them along, you will see a change in them that will astound you. If you are focusing on them like a true coach, you will help them grow to be more spiritual, kind, thoughtful, attentive, caring, loving, and so much more.

Your goal is to enjoy your family for an eternity, right? Focus on your eternal mate and coach them along as they coach you along and see what miracles happen in your lives. I know there will be struggles as you are coaching your mate, but you will have the satisfaction that you helped them past those difficulties and made them stretch beyond what they thought they were capable of. They need your help! You need their help! Each of you should step up and coach each other with the tools in this book. There will be times that you will say, "I can't do that." That's when your coach needs to step in and give you encouragement (not criticism) and help. They need to help you turn your weakness into strengths. Seek the guidance of the Holy Ghost to help you coach. Pray for help with ways to help your spouse. Pray together.

Above all, have faith in each other. As you use the tools within these pages you will have faith in each other to overcome that which you are having trouble with. I promise you that as you are sincere in using the tools in this book, you will turn those weak areas into strengths. The things you thought you couldn't do you will be doing. Have faith in your coach, your beloved eternal companion, and you will get through the hardest of times and become victorious.

In conclusion, remember to watch how your mate looks and acts when they are under the influence of Satan. Keep an eye out for your companion to help them through this mortal journey of life. Watch out for each other and work together in recognizing Satan and his influence. Cast Satan out from between you weekly, daily, hourly and every minute if necessary. Use the 9 point system to help your mate recognize and resolve negative situations. Rejoice together after you have conquered and then prepare for battle again. Become a trusted coach and friend. Together as you coach each other you will find new strength that you thought you never had. Be ready for Satan at all times. Remember that your relationship is what matters in this world and the world to come. You can't take anything else with you, but you can have your eternal mate for an eternity. Remember, you are stronger than Satan individually, but you are even a greater strength together.

HELPFUL TOOLS IDENTIFIED
OR EXPLAINED IN THIS CHAPTER:

1. Recognize your mate's attitude and demeanor.
2. The *stop stop stop* tool.
3. Set up ahead of time how you will use the *stop stop stop* tool.
4. Notice the attitude change from the pleasing to the harsh. Remember this for future reference.
5. Cast out Satan.
6. Use your faith.
7. Prayer.
8. Forgiveness.
9. Stop and assess your behavior when your mate uses the *stop stop stop* tool.
10. Discontinue conversation as long as one of you is under Satan's influence.
11. Recognize Satan's influence.

12. Remove Satan's influence.
13. Replace what you have removed with good positive thoughts.
14. Don't take it personally.
15. Separate your mate from the negative things that Satan is influencing them to say.
16. Recognize what your mate says is not of them.
17. Stay in control and don't become offended.
18. Speak in a soft loving tone of voice.
19. Sing a church hymn.
20. Read scriptures.
21. Discuss the situation with your mate and clear up any negativity between you.
22. Come up with a solution and resolve it totally.
23. Discuss what happened, how to avoid it in the future and what you will do if it happens again.
24. Forgiveness.
25. Victory song or dance.
26. Be grateful.
27. As you improve, adjust and set up a new game plan for future improvement.
28. Always look for new ways to improve.
29. Practice what you have learned or been asked to do.
30. Focus on coaching your eternal mate so that they can become all they can be.
31. Encourage your mate.
32. Seek the guidance of the Holy Ghost to help you coach your mate.
33. Pray together.

17

ARE YOU TAKING THE
PATH OF LEAST RESISTANCE?

There are many paths in this life in which to follow. Are you following a path or are you cutting a new path? Have you tried to blaze a new trail only to be stopped because of the difficulty of it? Did you turn back and continue on the same path you started from because it was easier? To set a path away from your comfort zone and into an area of self improvement will take some effort on your part. We will discuss what path you may be on and where this path will lead you. We will discuss what path you should be on and how to focus on your objective to accomplish what you have set out to do.

Let's say you are at the bottom of a mountain and your goal is to reach the top of it to witness the glory of the great view. Your goal may be to reach the top just to be able to say to someone, "I climbed to the top of that mountain once and the view was spectacular." You may just want to climb to the top to feel the accomplishment or just for the physical exercise. These are great goals and yet as you look up the mountain it is filled with treacherous trails, washed out paths, windy turns, steep ledges, slippery pebbles and rocks beneath your feet, hazards like snakes, bugs, prickly bushes, overgrown plants and the like. Each one of these things and many more you could be faced with before you get to the top.

"Yeah yeah yeah," I can see you saying to yourself, "I have heard this analogy before." Well good! How badly do you want a great relationship with your spouse? Isn't it exactly like climbing a mountain? Two people who live together, having been brought up in two different environments will most likely have to go through some trials. The difference is how you *go through* those trials. They don't have to be such huge trials that most people make them out to be. No matter how easy or hard your trials may be, remember this. You must pay the price for any worthwhile accomplishment. The only question is whether you are willing to pay the price to get it. The price will most likely be hard work, sacrifice, patience, persistence, and endurance.

As you work on things together and separately, you will find that it doesn't matter that the trail to the top is a little difficult. You won't mind if the snake slithered out onto your path and scared you. It won't be a big defeat if you are walking up the path and then you reach a slippery area and slide back down. You will find a way to persist to get back up to where you were again. The overgrown plants covering the path may slow you down but not stop your progress to the top. By using the tools in this book, you will lessen the pain of having to *go through* trials. In fact, you will be able to avoid some trials altogether. As you walk up the mountain you will have a tool to pick up that snake in your path and throw him out of your way. You will have the right shoes to gain traction so that you won't slip back down the mountain. You will have an ax, a shovel and a hedge trimmer to clear the bushes out of your path. Do you see what I am talking about? You will have the tools necessary for you to reach the top. Ok, I see you are getting this. Let's move on.

So what do I mean by the question, are you taking the path of least resistance? Most people would rather do what they are doing and do what they have always done. Does this sound like you? Are you stuck in always doing what you do and expecting others to change to fit your wants and needs? Do you always look to the other person and say, "If you had not done this, I would not have done that." Is change hard for you?

I believe that change is one of the hardest things for most of us to do. Unless you are truly dedicated in changing yourself for the better, it will not happen. You have to be open minded enough to evaluate your life and say to yourself, "I am not perfect. Why do I continue to think that I am perfect? Why do I expect others to conform to my life? Why do I feel this urge to have to be right?" If you evaluate the way you do things and interact with your spouse, you will see yourself in these profound questions.

You don't even have to answer these questions to see that it's all about you. This life is all about perfecting you, isn't it? How can you be perfect if you think you already are? When you are in denial and believe that you are perfect, you are not only denying yourself a better life and becoming a better person, but you are denying a better life for those around you. In reality, none of us are perfect, are we? None of us have attained the status of perfection like our Savior Jesus Christ. So look at yourself and decide that you want something better than you have right now and stop looking at others to change themselves to fit your desires, needs and wants. You are not perfect.

OK, with that said, let's look at you. Let's work on you. Let's say that you have been working on a particular issue that has been a weakness in the past. It is tough for you to overcome this weakness. It is like walking up that mountain and an overgrown bush gets in your way every few feet. It can be rather difficult as you walk every few feet and have to cut down or trim back another bush. You may start to get discouraged. You may start to think it is not worth it to get to the top of the mountain. This weakness you are overcoming may seem insurmountable. Then you say to yourself, "Self, this is too much. I am going to go back to the way I was because it is much easier than to overcome this weakness. I am tired of cutting back all these bushes." So, you turn around and start heading back the way you came until you find a new easier path that just goes around the mountain or even worse, it goes down instead of going up. This is not good.

> "Enter ye in at the strait gate: for wide *is* the gate, and
> broad *is* the way, that leadeth to destruction, and many
> there be which go in thereat: Because strait *is* the gate,
> and narrow *is* the way, which leadeth unto life, and

few there be that find it." (*Bible*, King James Version, Matthew 7: 13-14)

I like this scripture, because if you apply it to this situation you see that the path you need to follow is the straight gate and narrow way, which leadeth unto life. Continue up the narrow path to the straight gate at the top of the mountain. Don't be like everybody else. Most people will follow the road of least resistance and end up in the way that leadeth to destruction. This is Satan's way. Who do you think puts all those obstacles in your way as you are striving to the top? Well, Satan may not put them all there but I assure you that he certainly tries to make you as uncomfortable with those obstacles as he can. We put some of those obstacles in our own way by the choices we make. When we come upon these obstacles, Satan is right there tempting us to do the wrong things at the wrong time accentuating and blowing these challenges out of proportion as much as he can. Satan is whispering: *"This bush is too big to chop down. It is not worth cutting that bush out of our way because there will just be another one on the other side of it. Go back now before you hurt yourself. It was much easier when you didn't have this lofty goal. What's the use, you will never get to the top of the mountain anyway. Go down the mountain and be the way you were before, that way you won't have to struggle."*

Satan wants you to fail. He wants you to go down the path of least resistance. He wants you to be like water. Have you ever seen water drip from one place to another until it hits bottom. I have in my years seen many a roof leak where rain would come in through a hole or crack in the roof. It would start there and travel down the slope of the rafters until it came to a joint next to the ceiling of the house. It would then puddle up and drop even lower onto the ceiling drywall. After a while it would soak through and drip from the ceiling to a kitchen cabinet. There it would build up until it would find its way down the wall onto the counter top. Again it would puddle up and eventually find itself on the floor. Soon it would build up on the floor and spread throughout the house.

Do you see how Satan wants you to be like water? It's a slow but sure process that he wants you to follow. He wants to bring you down in stages as you follow the path of least resistance. Satan will bring you down so far until you get comfortable and then lead you down another step until you are comfortable there. This process is repeated as many times as it takes to get you where he wants you. With him!

Be like unto a tree in a thick forest. I have been in a jungle in South America where the trees were so thick I wondered how the little trees below would ever survive to be as big as the ones covering up the sun. A lot of them did survive but had to fight for the nutrition from the forest earth below and for the sunlight from above. They had to fight for the water that might only trickle down a little bit because the canopy above was catching all the water. Be like unto these little saplings who struggle and fight for everything they get for the chance to become a mighty tree! Eventually these trees get big and join the other trees so that they too can bask in the light of the sun. Just as you should fight against Satan and his tactics so that you too can bask in the light of the Son.

Where Do I Go For Help?

When you start feeling that you want to go back to the path of least resistance, start asking for assistance. You and your spouse should already be talking about what weaknesses the both of you have and have started a game plan on how you can help each other overcome them. This is a big area that will help you to keep your head up and to stop looking down. Work on ways to help each other especially when you feel discouraged. Make sure if you are the supporting spouse that you give comfort and aid to your discouraged spouse. Recognize the gains that have been made and point them out to them. Look at how far you have come. You are doing so well.

Don't say to the discouraged spouse, "If you hadn't have done this or that, you wouldn't feel that way." Don't say, "If you had done like I said, you wouldn't be in this situation." Those types of comments are really defeating and will only bring the discouraged spouse down even further. Don't point the finger. This is not how you will be a great strength together. Only say things that will uplift and support your spouse.

Another situation to avoid would be if the discouraged spouse says, "I am really working on this problem." Meanwhile, the other spouse is thinking or may even say, "Yeah, sure you are. You have failed at it three times this week. That doesn't look like you are working at it to me. I just don't see it." Don't fall into this trap of thinking the worst instead of thinking the best. What I mean by this is that the discouraged spouse may have had four victories and three failures this week. Wow, that's an improvement over the previous week of when they had six failures and one triumph. Yes there may still be room for improvement, but there has been improvement.

The way you can help the other spouse see your improvement is to talk about your successes. Linda and I have always done this. It really opens the other person's eyes to what is actually going on inside them.

Let me give you an example: Jim and Karen are really working on their weaknesses to turn them into strengths. Jim is working on not getting upset and angry when someone tells him to do something. He does not like being controlled. Even though the person that asks him to do something is not trying to be controlling, Jim is so sensitive about it, he thinks they are trying to control him and he gets upset about it. In the past, Jim would flare up about this issue an average of four times a week. He would blow up and make a scene or something that would cause everyone grief who was involved in the situation. Since Jim has been working on overcoming these emotional outbursts, this week he has only become upset two times. A couple of times this week at the kitchen table during dinner, Jim tells Karen about some instances at work where he could have flared up but didn't. He was able to keep under control two times this week. In addition, there was one time at home when he could have really flared up but kept control. Jim and Karen discussed this. Karen could see that Jim was trying as he said he would. Karen had also seen where he had flared up the other two times.

If Jim had not told Karen about any of the other times when he was under control, she would have little faith that Jim was actually trying to get this issue under control. Do you see what good communication can do for you? You should always talk about your triumphs as well as defeats. Sometimes you learn more when you are defeated as to how you can conquer it next time, but we all need to look at our victories as well. It is human nature to look at all the things your spouse is doing wrong and point those things out to them. Start climbing up the mountain instead of looking down the mountain. Look for those things that your eternal mate is doing right and praise them for it.

As in the example above, Karen should praise Jim for doing so well. She should encourage him to do better and tell him she is thankful he is putting forth his best efforts. She should appreciate his hard work. Don't forget, it is hard work for someone to overcome something that is engrained in them. Always give them positive feedback. This will help them tremendously.

You do need to watch how you give that feedback. This is the way the world says it, "Do unto others as you would have them do unto you." That's the Golden Rule, isn't it? Well, I don't like the Golden Rule as it is put here. I like to say, "Treat others as they would like to be treated." Another way to put this is, "Do unto others as they would like it done unto them." Do you notice the difference in the wording? Read the statements again. Not everyone would like to treated in the same way that you like to be treated. Everyone likes to be treated the way they like to be treated. Not everyone will like what you like or the way you like it. This is another reason for talking this out with your eternal mate. How do they like to receive praise and encouragement? Some people don't like to be doted over. Some just like to be patted on the back while saying, "Good job." Still others may just soak up every word of praise that you can give and want you to keep giving as much praise as you can. Discuss this and give each other praise the way they want and how they like it to be given to them.

Look At Your Eternal Companion In A Different Light!

Always uplift you eternal companion. As you lift up your companion, you are lifted up too. It's a team effort. How do you uplift and what does that actually mean? When you uplift your mate, you are helping them along the path to perfection. You do that by having unconditional love. Boy, that's a broad statement isn't it? That means that you should look past their weaknesses to see the real them. You accept that they have weaknesses and choose to look at who your mate is instead of what they do wrong. You have compassion on them enough to want to help them achieve their goals. If they fall down in their goals, you pick them up and encourage them to go on. You help them to see things from a different angle than they can see for themselves. You help them to realize that you are a team and that you will make it to the celestial kingdom together. All this is encompassed by your love and an understanding that it may not be easy. You only know it will be worth it.

In uplifting your mate, only look at their positive traits and admire them. When you are in conversation or just observing something your mate is doing, record in your mind this positive event. At the appropriate time, express to your mate the event or conversation that took place and then describe what good feelings you felt about it. Maybe it was something you admired about what they were doing or saying. It may be that at that moment they looked more beautiful to you than ever before. It could be that you felt the spirit rest upon them when they were talking to you. I guarantee that if you will think of the positive things your spouse does and really observe and seek after things to love about them, your love will increase toward them. Remove those negative things that most couples look for in their spouse so they can criticize them or cut them down. Focus on what positive things your mate does for you, the kids, at work, at home, at church, around other people, etc. If you will just tune in to the positive aspects your mate is capable of, you will have a better relationship than 90 percent of couples out there.

Put into practice uplifting your eternal mate and see what a difference it makes in your relationship. Ultimately, you will be looking at them in a different light. The light that shines on them will be glorious in your eyes and you will have a new vision of what and who they really are and what they are capable of. This will certainly help your mate up the mountain to success and keep them from looking back at the path of least resistance.

GEE, YOU HAVE A LOT OF ISSUES!

Wow, is that a statement or what? Don't get excited about it though. In some relationships, one spouse may have more weaknesses to overcome than the other. It may be an 80/20 mix where one spouse has more issues to overcome than the other. This just means that the 20 percent spouse has to be more patient than the 80 percent spouse. If you are concentrating on working as a team, it will be just as rewarding for the 20 percent spouse to help the 80 percent spouse to victory as it would to have a victory themselves.

The spouse that has more issues to overcome can sometimes feel overwhelmed by all the help they need. If this happens, they may want to quit. They see the other spouse always helping them and may start to feel guilty. They feel guilty that most of the concentration of effort is expended on them. They may even feel ashamed that they have more issues than the other spouse. They may feel like they are the bad guy all the time. Here again, that overwhelmed spouse just may think that they are not deserving of all this help. They may think that it's a waste of time to help them. They may think that they are a basket case and why should anyone help them. Negative thinking starts to enter into their mind. Self doubt and worry creep in there.

You really have to watch the negative thinking. Keep it under control. You know where it is coming from don't you? All this negative self talk comes from Satan's whisperings. He wants you to backslide into your old habits of doing what you have always done. He wants you to slide down the mountain enough times so that you will be discouraged. He wants you to turn around and follow the path of least resistance. Sometimes when someone gets into this mode, they fall into old habits and old thinking patterns. Satan wants you to play the blame game. You know the game. It's where everything is someone else's fault that you are miserable. Satan wants you to blame everyone else for your weaknesses instead of taking responsibility for your own behavior.

Satan wants you to respond negatively to your eternal mate with every excuse in the book as to why you are faltering on your commitment to improve yourself by overcoming your weaknesses. Satan will whisper to you things like, "*Why did my spouse say that to me? They know it irritates me when they do that.*" In all reality, your spouse may not know what irritates you if you have never told them it does. You start to make up things on a subconscious level that can reason away why you are failing to meet your goal of overcoming your weaknesses. You start to point the finger at everyone else for why you haven't made the gains you wanted to.

Ok, slow down. Work on one issue (weakness) at a time if you can. As the saying goes, Rome was not built in a day. Really work on one or two things you most want to overcome. So what if you have 80 percent of the issues between you both. Work on the worst ones first. Start whacking down those bushes in front of you one at a time as you work your way up the mountain to success. Once you have control over the worst ones, which should be the standard for you to look at and say, "If I can overcome that hurdle, the next ones should be a lot easier."

One of the ways to tackle these issues is to say positive affirmations. Say things like, "I am committed to overcoming this _____ problem. I love God and Jesus Christ and am doing whatever it takes to complete my mission. I am focused on overcoming this _____. The solution to overcoming this problem is _____. I love my husband/wife so much and want him/her to be happy with me. Overcoming this _____ is easy and long lasting. I am a fantastic husband/wife and appreciate my husband/wife for helping me overcome my weaknesses." Say these things or whatever affirmations that you can think of that will give you strength. Say them with emotion. Put your heart in it and really feel it as you say them.

It is best to say affirmations at minimum when you wake up in the morning and just before you go to bed at night. It is even better if you say affirmations during the day so that your morale is boosted all day long. Do not get discouraged that you have a lot of issues to work on. Just work on them the same way you would eat an elephant, one bite at a time. Don't get overwhelmed and stay focused.

Always remember it is a team effort. Don't get into the trap where the spouse who has only 20 percent of the issues gets tired of helping the one who has 80 percent of the issues. Don't get discouraged if you are the 80 percent spouse because the two of you are working on you more. You are in this together. The two of you should look at the whole picture. The two of you are 100 percent of the issues! It's really not about who has the most trials, temptations and challenges. It's about helping each other to reach your destination together. You need to help each other up the mountain. What good is it to reach the top of the mountain by your self? That's not what it is all about, is it? If fact, I don't think you could make it to the top without your mate. What do you think?

Remember, this life is worth the struggle to make it to the top of the mountain. You may or may not get to the top. Either way, it IS worth the struggle. As long as we are striving to make it to the top and are making progress along the way, the Lord will accept us. He knows where our heart is. If He sees that we are doing our best at climbing that mountain and putting in the effort as we help our mate along, do you think He will turn us away in the end because we didn't make it to the top? I think not. As long as we don't go down the path of least resistance as if we were water dripping from a leaky roof, He will be there to meet us in the end and congratulate us with a job well done. Be a tree in a forest that grows up taller and taller until you bask in the light of the Son.

Make sure you are supportive of one another's path toward overcoming each of your weaknesses. Notice even the smallest improvement as to your mate's progress in overcoming their weaknesses. Tell your mate about the times you overcame the temptations you had trouble with and let them see your victories. Help each other by uplifting your mate and not further discouraging the other by making negative remarks. Seek after positive things you see in each other and let that person know the positive things you were thinking about them. Don't get overwhelmed by looking at how many things there are for you to work on. Take one or two weaknesses at a time and work on them until you have overcome them. Then take on a couple more. Work together as a team and help each other up the mountain. As you put it all together from the things learned in this chapter your love will increase for each other and you will get excited to help one another. As you do these things while you are climbing up this mountain together and clearing the obstacles in your paths, you will find the inner strength to carry on as you become a great strength together.

Helpful Tools Identified
Or Explained In This Chapter:

1. Realize that you are not perfect.

2. Persistently fight against Satan.
3. Ask your spouse for assistance.
4. Give comfort and aid to your spouse by pointing out the gains your mate has made.
5. Don't point the finger at your spouse. Uplift and support them.
6. Talk about your successes and failures.
7. Praise your mate for the progress in overcoming their weaknesses and the things they are doing right.
8. Thank your mate for putting forth their best effort.
9. Appreciate your mate.
10. Show unconditional love by accepting your mate's weaknesses.
11. Look at who your mate is and not what they are doing wrong.
12. Have compassion on your mate.
13. Help your mate see things from a different perspective.
14. Realize that you and your mate are a team and it takes a team effort.
15. Seek after things to love about your mate.
16. Work on one or two issues at a time.
17. Use positive affirmations.
18. Be persistent and stay focused on overcoming your weaknesses.

18
ARE YOU A PART OF MY WORLD?

What world are you a part of? Do you have your own little world where you are doing your thing and your mate is doing their thing? Do you bring your eternal companion into your world? What do I mean by *your world?*

Each of us has a little world around us. Our world is everything we come in contact with, invite, communicate with and use our five senses to experience. Things that may or may not be included in our world would be: our spouse, our kids, parents, job, co-workers, church, callings, our home, our vehicles, sports, school, any activities we enjoy, video games or TV, clubs, volunteer groups, cooking, etc. This is a short list and of course there are thousands of things that could be in our world.

Who or what do you let into your world? Is your eternal mate included in your world? "Oh," you say, "of course my eternal companion is included in my world." But are they really? Do you involve them in what you are doing? I hope the answer is yes. I think that most couples are at least aware of what is in their spouse's world. What about you being in their world? Are you interested in what they are doing and what's going on in their world? I am not quite sure you know the importance of all these questions. Do you?

This is another very important building block to a successful eternal companionship. Some couples have the idea that as long as they are together while they are doing *their own thing* that all is well. Some couples don't really communicate very well in this area and tend to shut their mate out of certain parts of their world. I think this is a vital mistake.

Let me give you an example: Larry and Edna happen to be a so called happily married couple. She is a big fan of scrap booking. Larry just loves to play golf. Every Saturday Larry goes golfing with his buddies. He spends the whole day playing golf and talking with his friends. On Tuesday and Thursday evenings, Edna is out with her friends scrap booking. Neither one of them even talked about their spouse to their friends. Neither one of them communicated with each other about what they did during those events. They just go on with life as if nothing ever happened on Tuesday, Thursday and Saturday. It was just a blank hole in their lives so to speak.

OK, so you say, "Well duh, Larry probably doesn't like scrap booking and Edna probably doesn't like to golf. So what?" OK, I'll give you that. I do not believe they have to like each others activities, but I do believe that they should talk about them to each other. Invite your spouse into your world to share your desires, accomplishments and dreams. Larry should share with Edna what he talked about with the guys or how he got a birdie on the sixth hole. Now Edna may be bored stiff about the game of golf, but she should show some interest in how her husband feels as he is telling her. Share his excitement or his pain. This is about sharing with each other. Feeling a part of each others lives. Likewise Edna should share with Larry what she did and how she felt and what they talked about. Larry, wake up! Show some interest in your wife. Scrap booking may be boring for you but look into your wife's eyes and see how happy it makes her and share that moment with her.

ARE YOU TOGETHER OR NOT?

The idea of separatism is truly disturbing to me. If there is no sharing with one another there can be no togetherness. Yes, you may say, "Yeah, but they share other things with each other, don't they?" Maybe so and maybe not. A couple is either together or they are not. It is this open communication that keeps the relationship healthy. If a man or woman shows no interest in their mate's world, it sends a strong message that they are not interested in them! Couples need to be interested in what their mate is doing in everything or it could become habit to not be interested in anything.

I think couples start to drift apart when they are not interested in certain parts of their companion's world. If they are not interested in one thing, it becomes easier to not be interested in something else. As things add up, they become totally disinterested in anything their spouse does. You do not want to go there now do you? Of course not. So get interested!

How do you feel when someone is interested in what you are doing? It makes you feel good doesn't it? Think about it. Have you ever talked to a complete stranger about something that you were interested in? As they showed interest in what you were talking about, didn't you feel an affinity for them? You liked that person because they were interested in what you were talking about. Guess what? This goes for your companion as well don't you think?

So, I can hear you saying, "That all sounds good, but what if I am really not interested in hearing what my spouse has to say about scrap booking or whatever? I just think it is a waste of time." Well, to that I must say that a waste of time it is not! You may not like to hear about something that your mate is interested in, but you are interested in your mate aren't you? You better be if you are planning on being a celestial couple. So, it looks like you may need an attitude adjustment.

This is not about wasting your time. Your time is not wasted when you are listening to your mate intently as they tell you about their world. It's about you being a part of their world and them being a part of your world. It is about unity and having oneness. This will keep you close. As your mate is telling you about their day don't just think in your head, "This is really boring. I don't want to hear this. Can't he/she think of something else to talk about? I can't wait until they are done with this subject." Stop right now. Don't think those negative thoughts. Try to understand what they are telling you. Be interested in what they are saying. Ask them questions and truly be interested. This may take effort on your part I know. It is worth it. Treat your mate with respect as you show your interest. You may be surprised to find out that you may really get interested in what they are doing just by showing interest. The following is an example of what Linda and I have done to show interest.

Linda is a first grade teacher. She goes to school every day and gets to deal with about thirty little children. Each of those children has their own issues going on in their life. It is quite a handful for any teacher. When she comes home in the evening, I ask her how her day went. She has a different story to tell me every day. As Linda tells me about a specific incident I listen intently. Most of the time, these stories revolve around two or three children. As she describes her day and tells me about these children I listen so that I will remember what their names are and what is happening with them. This is very important to know if I want to be a part of Linda's world. If I just listened and didn't ask questions or participate in the discussion, I might as well be a brick wall for Linda to talk to.

So, she tells me about one little boy named Angel. At the beginning of the school year he just sits at his desk leaning back and says, "I am bored. I don't want to be here. I don't know how to read. I don't want to read. This is boring." He was a little bit of a problem for Linda because he would not participate at first. Each day Linda would come home and tell me about Angel. She would tell me how she worked with him, what his issues were and how she helped him overcome them. Within two weeks, Angel was excited to read and would ask Linda if he could help the other children with their reading. He even presented her with a card that said, "To the best teacher. Thanks for teaching me to read." I would listen to Linda tell me each evening about his progression. I showed interest by asking questions. Some evenings I would simply ask Linda, "How is Angel doing today?" Linda would perk up and get excited to tell me the news of the day. Linda told me that the way she brings me into her world is not only to tell me about what happened to her that day, but she talks about me to the children.

Linda said that one time she told Angel, "I told my husband about how well you are doing and he was excited and happy that you are doing so well." Another time she announced to the class, "My husband told me that I should use this megaphone today." Linda has a special electronic megaphone that transforms her voice into several electronic weird sounding voices. It's a fun way to break up the monotony and give a little comic relief for the restless little children. If I hadn't known anything about her world and what she does, I wouldn't have known about the megaphone and she wouldn't have mentioned anything to the kids.

Through the experiences of Linda telling me about her world, I became interested enough that I actually visited her class a couple of times. Now the students had a face to attach to Linda's husband and I had little faces to attach to Linda's stories.

I hear what you are probably thinking. You may think, "This is no big deal. So what?" Here is what I think. Sometimes it seems that during waking hours we are away from our spouse more than we are together with them. This is because one or both of you are working and traveling to and from work. This takes up most of the day. Wouldn't it be nice to bring your eternal mate along with you to work? I realize that this is not always possible depending upon the job that you have, but if there was a way to include your spouse like the way Linda included me in talking to her students, it might help you stay closer to them. You would be thinking about your eternal mate in order to include them, right?

So, in this example several things happened. Can you pick them out? OK, I will help you. As Linda would describe her day to me I would listen. This helped Linda to feel that I cared about what she was doing with her life. I showed enough interest that I asked questions and remembered what she had told me previously so I would be kept up to date with what was going on. Linda knew I was interested in her world because I did this. Linda felt loved, appreciated and connected to me. Next, since Linda and I would discuss her class, she could talk to her class about what I had said and bring me into her world. Linda felt like I was part of her world as she talked about me to the children. This made her feel closer to me by bringing me into the classroom with her. She was thinking about me. Then, when Linda would come home, we would discuss her day. She would tell me that she mentioned me to her class today. The fact that she brought me into her classroom and told the kids something I had said made me feel a part of her world. It made me feel loved appreciated and connected to her.

Do you see what I mean? If we intertwine our lives together and show true interest in what is happening in the others life, our love will grow and not falter. Do you think I wanted to hear about a bunch of little kids every evening? Not really. What I really wanted to do was to be interested in my eternal companion. How I did it was to listen to what she had to say. As she talked about the kids in her class, I became interested. As she involved me, I became even more interested. I enjoy talking to her about her class and am grateful to be included in her world. Of course, I also tell her about my day and she is interested in my world as well.

This is a tool in this book that you need to use every day. Be interested in your spouse's world. When you are, you are showing your love for them. Women, even if you are not interested in how he rebuilt the engine in the car he is restoring, listen and try to understand what he is doing. You may not know how to rebuild a carburetor but you can experience the enthusiasm of your husband as he tells you about it. Men, even though you may not be interested in the mundane things your wife did with the kids today, it is important to her that you listen and be a part of her world. As you become a part of each others world and show interest in being a part of it, you will learn more about each other. This will do well to help you feel loved, appreciated and connected with your eternal mate. This will help you to progress as the celestial couple as you become a great strength together.

Helpful Tools Identified
Or Explained In This Chapter:

1. Share your desires, accomplishments and dreams with your mate as you bring them into your world.
2. Show interest as your mate shares their world with you.
3. Openly communicate with your mate about what is happening in each others world.

4. Listen intently as your mate tells you about their world.
5. Do not think negative thoughts while your mate is telling you about their world.
6. Try to understand what your spouse is telling you.
7. Treat your mate with respect as you show interest.
8. Ask questions to show your interest.
9. Bring your mate into your world mentally, emotionally and or physically if possible.

19

I Compliment You!

How well do you take compliments? Does it matter who is giving the compliment? What do you think about it once it is given? Do you discount it or shine within because it makes you feel good? Do you give compliments? How often?

This is a subject which on the surface seems so easy to understand that it may not be worth discussing. On the surface it would seem that if someone compliments another person, the one receiving the compliment feels good and goes on with life. They may even feel an affinity for the one giving the compliment. OK, subject over, right? Not so. It goes much deeper than that.

Compliments can be taken many ways with the various personalities that we have. Some people like compliments. Some seek after them. Others may dislike anyone who gives them a compliment. While some people are embarrassed by compliments, others think that someone is manipulating them into doing something. There are many different ways to feel about a compliment, don't you agree?

Compliments in general are good for one's soul. The first thing you should know about compliments is how to give them. They should be given freely without someone expecting them. They should be given from the heart. Positive feelings should be running through your mind about whom you are complimenting. It will be only natural that what you say will be positive. You don't have to be overly complimentary to get your point across. Simple compliments are the best as long as they come from the heart.

Compliments are for building someone up. You have to be honest with your compliments. Give them with sincerity. Mean what you say and say what you mean. If you give out compliments and really don't mean what you say, you will be found out by those receiving it from you and soon they will discount everything you say. Don't let this happen to you. You can be a great inspiration for people if you follow some simple rules I will lay out for you as we go along.

When you are sincere in complimenting people, especially your eternal mate, they will gain a confidence in what you say. Their self esteem will grow and be of benefit to them. Everyone needs more self confidence and the approval of others whether they know it or not. Some people exude self confidence and yet they need the approval of others to justify their confidence. These types of people should give out more compliments than they receive because this strengthens the receivers. What better compliment could be received than from someone with a lot of self confidence?

How should a compliment be given? It is best to give it in a positive way with nothing negative mixed in. Here is an example of what you should say. "That is a pretty dress you have on." This is what you should not say. "That dress you have on looks better than that other ugly dress you were going to put on." Do you see the difference? If you are going to give a compliment, give one. Don't drag something negative into it where it doesn't belong. As in the example of the negative compliment, the dress that looks better than the ugly dress is not much of a compliment. She could be thinking many different things about that statement like, "How much better than the ugly dress is the dress I have on? Is it only slightly better or much better? What about the ugly dress? Why does he think that dress is ugly? I like it." On and on with the questioning mind it goes bringing in more doubt and anxiety about what she is wearing. With the first and positive compliment, she may think only positive things like, "This is a pretty dress and I am glad he likes it. It makes me feel good that he thinks this dress is pretty.

I am glad I picked this dress out to wear." On and on with positive thoughts, which brings positive feelings and builds self confidence. What a difference, right?

The old adage is, "If you can't think of anything positive to say, then don't say anything at all." I think this applies greatly to our relationship with our spouses. Everyone has the ability to see good things in their spouse and compliment them on it. Everyone has good qualities if you look hard enough. Even in the hardest and coldest relationships, if you really look for something positive in someone else, you will find something to compliment them on. Hopefully your relationship has not gone into that realm where you have to look long and hard at your eternal companion to find something positive. I am betting that you can see the good things about your mate rather easily.

We all need a pat on the back occasionally. Some of us thrive on compliments because it is the way we feel loved. Now that we have talked about how we should give compliments, let's move into the more complicated realm of how we should receive them.

RECEIVE THEM GRACIOUSLY

As I said earlier, there are many ways to receive a compliment. The best way to receive one is to take it at face value. Don't try to read into it more than is there. Sometimes people will hear the compliment and think to themselves, "What did she mean by that when she said she thought my tie looks nice with this suit? I wonder if the tie I wore last week looked bad." Another example might be, "The way he told me he like's my hair makes me feel like maybe he didn't like my hair before." These are counterproductive thoughts. You must do only one thing with these types of thoughts. Get rid of them!

First of all, when you are trying to read something negative into what the other person complimented you about you are negating the compliment. You are, in your mind, not accepting the compliment. You are immediately discounting what was said and thinking something negative about what the other person's intentions are. How can you be built up with a compliment if you tear it right down from the start? The number one purpose of a compliment is to build up the receiver. To let them know they are appreciated. To let them know that someone cares about them. To let them know that what they do or say is meaningful and noticed by others. It validates their value. So when you immediately think something negative when someone has complimented you, you are not allowing someone to build you up. You are tearing down that person's opportunity to help you. You have the need to feel loved don't you? You want to feel good about yourself too, right? Of course you do. We all do. So let go of the negative self talk that only defeats the purpose of your feeling better about who you are.

Secondly, when you use this negative self talk, you are causing feelings of doubt and resentment toward someone who has just tried to build you up. How disheartening is that? Having negative feelings or doubts about someone who is on your side. This can get in the way of your relationship. It can be like building a brick wall. Wow, how did I get from accepting compliments to building a brick wall?

It is as simple as this. There are many things that happen in your life both positive and negative. Unfortunately, human nature is such that in most people, the negative out ways the positive by about ten to one. In other words, a person needs to hear ten positive statements about themselves to override one negative comment. And in reverse, if someone hears ten positive comments about themselves, it will only take one negative comment to tear that all down. If you look at each negative comment as being one brick in a wall that you are building between you and your eternal mate, you can soon see how this analogy rings true. With each negative comment, or thought of negativity towards your spouse, you are adding one brick to that wall between you. How fast do you want to build that wall? Personally, I do not want any sort of wall there at all. You should be thinking the same thing. This is because with each brick of negativity that is placed there, it takes ten positive comments, actions or thoughts to take that brick out. There is much more work involved to take that brick out than there is to not put it there in the first place. Do you see what I mean? Don't go there!

Stop all the negative self talk and accept the compliment for its face value. There are only two words that you should use to accept a compliment. Do you know what they are? Of course you do. The two words that you should accept every compliment with are, "Thank you." Accept and move on by thinking positive thoughts about the one complimenting you. Thank you really says a lot. It acknowledges the person giving the compliment so that they feel validated. Now they feel good about giving the compliment and are likely to continue to give you compliments in the future. What if you had squashed their compliment by saying something like, "How could you think that?" What if you said, "Oh, you are just saying that because that's what you are supposed to do." How do you think that would make them feel? They would probably feel like they were sorry they even gave you the compliment, right? Then you would likely not receive very many compliments after that because you had not accepted them graciously. You see how this helps both the giver and the receiver?

DISCOUNTING COMPLIMENTS

One of the most common errors in this process I would like to address is the act of discounting your family's compliments. This occurs among spouses, children and parents. We tend to discount the positive comments of all those family members who are close around us. I have heard kids say to a parent after their compliment to the child, "You are my mom. You are supposed to say that." This comment is a little disturbing to me. Comments from a wife who says after a compliment from her husband, "Husbands are supposed to compliment their wives, but I still think I look fat in this dress." These types of negative and defeating comments about the compliment from a close family member are typical and should be avoided. What I find interesting is that most people will accept what the *world* tells them rather than what a family member tells them. Most people will discount what a family member compliments them on because they feel that it is expected. I expect you to say that because you are my family and that is just what families are supposed to do, right? They will accept what a non family member tells them faster than their closest family member. This is sad because the world is getting to be so worldly and for us to be accepted by the world is a tragedy in itself. We need to train ourselves to accept the family's compliments more than the world. The trick here is balance.

Balance out your compliments to each other. Don't give them out like raindrops during a storm. Don't hide them like water in a desert on a hot summer day. Look for something that you truly see that your spouse is making an effort on and compliment that. Seek for opportunities to point out good qualities in your mate. Seek for opportunities to build up your spouse in an area that they are weak. This can be the most difficult of all, but the most rewarding.

Let me give you an example: Ever since Linda and I have been married, I have known that when she was a child, her parents treated her very badly. Her father would call her dumb and stupid along with a few colorful expletives. She was constantly barraged with this type of negative treatment all while she was growing up. She figured that because her parents said she was dumb and stupid all the time, and she not knowing any better as a kid, that she must be. So since she thought she was dumb and stupid, why bother to learn anything. She did learn a lot even though she didn't think she did. Linda learns quickly but hasn't recognized it in herself.

So, with this as a background on Linda, I quickly sought out opportunities to point out to her how smart she is. A certain situation would happen and she told me how she resolved it. I saw the wisdom in what she had done and quickly told her how smart she was for handling it that way. Another time we were in a discussion and she came up with an idea that was great and I told her how smart she was for coming up with that idea. Linda has helped tremendously with this book in coming up with ideas to help you have a better relationship with your eternal mate. I have told her how smart she is by giving me ideas as I write this book. Because I want to help her overcome all the negative programming she had when she was a kid, I am always looking for opportunities to compliment her on how smart she is.

At first, this was foreign to her. She discounted it and made fun that I was saying she was smart. After so many years of hearing how dumb and stupid she was, it was hard for her to take my positive comments seriously. I find it amazing how well she has done in her life considering how she was brought up and the mental abuse she went through. My compliments would stir up some of the negative emotions she felt as a child, which made it hard for her to accept what I was saying to her. As I would find more and more opportunities to tell her how smart she was, she began to accept them more and more. She started to see how smart she really is and this has helped her. This has sparked a new confidence in her she has never had before. Do you see how you can use the power of compliments to build someone up and make a difference in their life? Good! Now let's take this another step.

COMPLIMENT PROGRESS

As you see progress in something your mate is working on, you need to recognize it and give a compliment about it. For example, let's say your spouse is working on not yelling when they are angry. Let's say a month goes by and you see a significant reduction of flare ups. You need to recognize that and give a compliment to your spouse for not yelling as many times as they did the last month. You should notice the progress because you should have already talked about this with your spouse before hand. You should know what issues they are working on so that you can both help each other. Keep a sharp eye out for their progress and compliment them on it. This will do two things.

First, it will keep you aware that they are making a concerted effort and you will be able to see their progress. Second, it will help your spouse to know that you recognize they are making an effort and are making headway. This gives them the strength to continue to move forward until this issue is overcome. Like I said before, everyone needs a pat on the back to say a job well done for their efforts.

So compliment them even if you see just a little effort or a little progress. Tell them that you see progress and you see their efforts. Do this especially at the time when you see the effort or the progress. Say, "I see you are making the effort to _____. I see your progress. In the past, you used to _____. This time you didn't. Thank you for the effort of bettering yourself and improving our eternal marriage." This will help encourage them to continue.

If they don't get your recognition and encouragement, they will likely stop and say to themselves, "My spouse doesn't even recognize that I am making an effort. They don't even see my progress. What does it matter then? I might as well stop." You get the point I am trying to make, don't you?

Compliments should come from the heart and be truthful and honest. As you do this, you will be less likely to discount what the other family member says because you know it is from the heart. Give compliments regularly and don't be stingy with them. Seek after ways to build up your eternal mate with compliments when you see improvement in overcoming their weaknesses. Help them build those weaknesses up to be strengths and this will bring you satisfaction as well. Accept compliments as they were given without reading anything negative into them. This will keep you in harmony with the giver of the compliment. Accept the compliments from your family and especially your mate. Because you are giving compliments from the heart, you should accept them as the gift they are. Leave the negative comments and thoughts out of your life so that you don't build that brick wall between you. Remember it takes ten positive compliments to tear down one negative comment. As you compliment each other in a positive manner and focus on each other to build one another up, I promise you that your relationship will grow tighter and tighter together as you become a great strength together.

HELPFUL TOOLS IDENTIFIED
OR EXPLAINED IN THIS CHAPTER:

1. Compliments should be given freely without someone expecting them.
2. Give compliments in a positive manner.
3. Give honest and sincere compliments.
4. Receive compliments graciously by saying thank you.
5. Receive compliments at face value. Believe them.
6. Do not let counterproductive negative thoughts enter your mind when receiving a compliment.
7. Think positively about the one giving you a compliment.
8. Accept compliments from family members more than from the world.
9. Seek opportunities to build up your spouse with compliments.
10. Recognize progress in your mate and compliment them on it.

20
WHAT IS THE APPRECIATION GAME?

As you are going through your day, what thoughts do you have about your eternal mate? Are they good thoughts or are you thinking of what they did yesterday that irritated you? How often do you think of your spouse? Are you thinking thoughts of appreciation or thoughts of retaliation? Are you thinking of ways to control your lover or are you thinking of how you can work with them for the benefit of the two of you?

Your relationship will be determined by the way you think and feel about your wife or husband. If you think negative things about your mate, you will only see the negative things about them. Conversely, if you think positive things about your mate, you only see the good things in them. The same is true about what you attract into your life. If you think negatively you will attract negative things into your life. If you think positively you will attract positive things into your life. I want you to start thinking positive things about your eternal companion each day. I especially want you to think positive things about them after you have had a disagreement. This will be one of the hardest things for you to do but the benefits will pay out big time.

There are several ways to do this but I am going to suggest getting into a habit at a certain time of day in a certain place that will trigger you to think that way. We are all creatures of habit. If we develop good habits like the one I will describe here, you will reap huge benefits down the road. This is what works for me. I get up in the morning and take a shower. While I am in the shower it doesn't take much thought to wash myself and shampoo my hair (what little hair I have). So I use this time to think positive thoughts about my true love Linda. I usually think of something that she did or said that made me feel good. It may be something simple like the way she hugs me. I think about the smile she has on her face when she sees me. Today as I write this I was thinking of how we handled a certain situation last evening. We are always working on everything that I have written about in this book. Last evening was no different.

The next morning I was in the shower thinking about how we used the tools contained in this book to resolve the situation of the previous evening. I was thinking of how special Linda was as we worked through the situation. I was also thinking of how nice it is to hug her. When I got out of the shower and got dressed, I found Linda and gave her a big hug. I then told her, "I was just thinking in the shower of how special you are. I just wanted you to know that I appreciated the way you were able to be open minded and release the negative past and replace it with the correct perception." Linda said, "Wow, you are nice. I was just thinking about how special you are and how you appreciate me."

My point here is that you should pick a time and or place that you think about your spouse in a positive manner. I use the shower for my *trigger* to think and appreciate different things that I love about my eternal mate. It may be that your thinking time could be on your drive to work or while you are eating your breakfast. It could be while you are rocking your baby to sleep or combing your hair. Pick a time or event or something that will trigger you to think about your eternal companion. Be regular about it. Think positive thoughts only! Dislodge the negative thoughts from your mind. Satan wants you to think that way. He wants you to tear down your spouse in your mind. Satan wants you to think those negative thoughts about your spouse so that he can influence you to do or say something negative that will hurt your relationship. So take the time to think of good stuff. You should actually think of ways that you appreciate them.

What kind of things can I think about, you ask? You won't have to look very far to see the good things your spouse says or does. Don't take anything for granted. Start noticing the little things you like or enjoy about your spouse. It may be that you like the way they brush their hair away from their face. It could be the way they hug you or play with the children. It might be the way she crosses her legs, the way he smiles, how she says hello when you get home, the way he cares about your day, the way she reads out loud, the way he works so hard to make a living, the way she takes care of the kids, etc. You get the point?

I am not sure you do. Some things are really obvious that we can appreciate about our spouse but other things that should be obvious are not obvious enough for us to go out of our way to tell our spouse we appreciate them. I am going to tell you some of the not so obvious things that some people take for granted. Do you appreciate your spouse because they take care of themselves physically, groom themselves neatly, pay the bills on time, take the kids to school, changed the oil in the car, prepares dinner, goes grocery shopping, washes the clothes, etc. Every mundane thing that we all do yet no one notices because it is expected. Forget expected and show appreciation!

Think of the positive things each and every day at least once per day and preferably five or more times throughout the day. Don't just think of one thing each time. Think of as many as you can in the time that you have. As you get into the habit of thinking positive thoughts it will be harder for the negative thoughts to creep in there.

Once you are in the habit of thinking about the great and marvelous things you love about your mate, I want you to start verbalizing your thoughts. Tell your spouse what you were thinking about today. Show appreciation to your spouse about what you were thinking as I did in the example above. Tell them that you appreciate them because _____ (fill in the blank). Showing appreciation for something that someone does is one of the highest forms of showing love. It is also one of the biggest motivators to perpetuate good behavior. If someone does not feel appreciated for what they do, they may stop doing it because they may feel that since no one does appreciate them for it, why do it.

Take nothing for granted. Showing appreciation is very important in your relationship. It is also just as important to thank your spouse for appreciating you. Do not just brush off the appreciating spouse by saying something like, "Oh that's nothing. That's not anything great. I do that anyway whether you like it or not." Do not say anything negative, just accept the comment and appreciate that your spouse has thought something about you that they appreciate. Thank them positively. This will do five things for you and your eternal mate:

1. It will let your mate know you were thinking about them.
2. It will let them know that you appreciate them.
3. It will get them to start thinking more about you if they haven't already.
4. They will want to verbalize the positive things about you that they were thinking.
5. This positive feedback will generate more positive feelings toward your mate and will cause you to think more about your spouse in return.

This is a positive circle that I refer to as The Appreciation Game. I have already described all the steps in the appreciation game. Here are the steps in case you missed them:

1. Set up a time of day or event that you will regularly spend time thinking positive things about your mate. These things can span from simple to big things.
2. Once you have a list of things in your mind that you enjoy and appreciate about your mate, verbalize those thoughts to them.
3. Tell your mate what you were thinking about them and express your gratitude and appreciation for what you were thinking about. Do this every day.
4. Thank the appreciating spouse. If so inspired you may also appreciate them right back. This game can be quite contagious.

The more you think of new ways to show gratitude and appreciate your eternal companion, the more ways that your eternal companion will think of ways to be grateful and appreciate you. Even in the face of disagreements you can find positive things you can focus on. It is better to feel good about your mate and be happy than it is to be right. In the appreciation game, everyone wins.

A shortened version of the appreciation game may be played at any moment. This works really well when you are doing something together or just talking to one another. It works like this. When your spouse least expects it, stop and say to them something like, "I really love the way you smile." Another comment might be, "You are so cute when you are talking that way." Just say something nice that your mate is not expecting you to say. It kind of throws them off guard. It's a pattern interrupt that makes them stop and think, "My eternal mate is so nice to say that about me. He/she really loves me and cares about me." This especially works well if you kiss them after you have appreciated them.

All throughout your life, Satan will be whispering negative thoughts to you to think bad things about your eternal mate. One way to bounce Satan's negative whisperings out of your mind is to think about all those positive thoughts about your mate. Also, think about all the positive things they said to you and how they appreciated you. Get those positive thoughts flowing in your mind. Purge Satan's whisperings from your mind. Remember to recognize Satan's whisperings, remove them from your mind and replace them with those positive thoughts about your eternal companion. This is just another powerful tool to help you and your mate have victories over the adversary.

Concentrate on your eternal mate and the positive things about them that make you happy. Show your appreciation by verbally expressing it to each other often. Use those positive thoughts to win the victory over Satan's fiery darts that seek to destroy you and your eternal mate's happiness. If you are both thinking along those lines and stop thinking those negative thoughts that most of the world thinks and think positive thoughts about your mate, you will be so much happier and will be a great strength together.

HELPFUL TOOLS IDENTIFIED
OR EXPLAINED IN THIS CHAPTER:

1. Think positive things about your eternal mate.
2. Appreciate your mate.
3. Be open-minded.
4. Pick a regular time and or place to think positive thoughts about your eternal mate.
5. Dislodge any negative thoughts about your mate.
6. Notice little things that you like or enjoy about your mate.
7. Appreciate even the mundane things your mate does and let them know about it.
8. Kiss your mate after you have told them how you appreciate them.
9. Think about all the positive things your mate said to you and how they appreciated you.
10. Recognize the negative whisperings from Satan
11. Remove the negative whisperings from Satan from your mind using the tools in this book.
12. Replace those thoughts in your mind with positive thoughts about your eternal companion.

21

Victories!

As we go through our daily routines, we will have various struggles within ourselves and with our spouse. I guarantee that as you use the tools in this book, you will get better at recognizing Satan's influence upon your life. You will see the various angles he uses to drive wedges between a husband and wife. At times you will be frustrated and possibly angry as you discover Satan's tactics. Remember, Satan has had thousands of years to perfect his battle plan. You are just now discovering these highly thought out attacks on you and your spouse.

As you use the tools in this book more and more you will find new ways to have victories. Each time you discover one of Satan's tactics and overcome it or defeat it, you need to make note of it. Make no mistake about it; this *is* a war with the adversary. In times of war, one needs to keep track of the victories and defeats. How else does one know whether they are winning or loosing the war? The war is won by defeating the enemy more times than you lose. You do this one battle at a time.

It is easy to get discouraged when Satan is messing with you so much to get you to do or say the wrong thing. Sometimes it may feel overwhelming. I have found a couple of ways that you can boost the morale of the troops, so to speak. This will help you feel better about continuing. One way to do this is to carry some 3x5 cards around with you. On a 3x5 card make two columns. At the top of one column write the heading "Attacks" and on the other write "Victories."

Each time you feel that Satan attacked you by making you feel down, or tempted you to do something or say something, put a hash mark under the Attack side. Every time you withstood the temptation or whispering to do or say something, put a hash mark on the Victories side. Make a hash mark on the victories side even if you have a partial victory. A partial victory you might want to rank on a scale of one to ten, one being no victory and ten being complete victory. For example, let's say that you normally get mad at someone and blow up at them. This would be a one on the scale. A partial victory would be if you got mad but were able to keep under control and not blow up. This might be a four or five on the scale. Improvement is improvement and you must make note of it. Obviously you will be working on getting a ten victory every time. Keeping track of your victories will accomplish a couple things for you.

First, it will bring more awareness to your mind about Satan's attacks because you are keeping track. Secondly, you will begin to see how many victories you have actually had. Some days may not be so good and some may be fantastic. Either way, you need to see that you are having victories. This will help you to see where you are and how you are improving.

Speaking of improving, as you are watching your improvement, you may notice that you did not get so mad this time or that your reaction wasn't quite as severe as last time or that this time you felt more positive. You may have done something just a little bit different this time. You caught yourself half way through a harmful statement and stopped before you got it all out. Maybe you said the full statement but quickly asked for forgiveness from the person you said it to. These are signs that you are beginning to change for the better. These are victories and should be counted as such. You need to see improvement! This will give you encouragement to continue to get better at overcoming these temptations you are having trouble with.

Help your spouse recognize the improvements. Tell each other what a great job they are doing when you notice that a certain behavior has changed for the better. A simple example would be a husband who 90 percent of the time forgets to take out the trash. The wife constantly reminds him to take it out. What if the husband was remembering to take it out even 50 percent of the time? Would this not be a noticeable improvement? The wife should say something like, "I have noticed that you have been remembering to take the trash out more often. I appreciate that and want to thank you." Do you think that would make a greater impact on the husband and help him to remember more often than 50 percent? I think it would. The more often you appreciate your mate when you see improvement, the more improvement will occur.

Another thing that will help you tremendously is to reward yourself for those victories. After Satan has beat down on you as you do battle with him, you need something to lift your spirits. I have found that singing a church hymn is just what the spirit needs. You will be amazed at how this will bring you up and stay with you.

As I mentioned earlier, a great hymn that Linda and I love to sing is "Behold! A Royal Army" (*Hymns, N. 251*). Actually, we just sing the chorus. It goes like this:

> Victory, victory, through Him that redeemed us.
> Victory, victory, through Jesus Christ our Lord.
> Victory, victory, victory,
> Through Jesus Christ our Lord.

We sing this many different times depending what the situation is. We may sing it after we add up our totals for the day or week on our little Attack/Victories card. We may sing it after we have had a big victory where Satan has tried to drive a wedge between us. Sometimes if we feel a little bit down and want to get rid of the gloomy feeling, we will sing the victory song, as we call it.

What really makes it nice is to sing it with your spouse. Linda and I face each other and hold hands as we sing. Then on the last part where we sing, "Victory, victory, victory…," we raise our hands high in the air as we sing with big smiles on our faces.

Now, you can sing whatever hymn or song that you want. Whatever gives your spirit a lift. Sing something that makes you happy. Singing it with your spouse will help that bond grow tighter. These types of things usually don't go over well with you macho guys, but trust me, you will come to love doing this with your wife while looking into her smiling face and seeing how happy it makes her.

Keep track of your victories throughout the day on your scorecard. This is a way to keep track to know that you are improving. It also helps you to be aware of Satan's attacks so you can correct them. Add up the totals of your victories and celebrate! Sing the victory song or whatever song you feel that will help you to feel good inside. Celebrate with your mate whenever possible. As you do these things together with your mate and see your victories as you go, the two of you will bond together as you become a great strength together.

Helpful Tools Identified
Or Explained In This Chapter:

1. Keep track of your victories and defeats on a 3X5 scorecard.
2. Forgiveness.
3. Help your spouse recognize improvements.
4. Tell each other what a great job you are doing.
5. Appreciate your mate.
6. Reward yourself for victories over Satan.
7. Sing a church hymn.
8. Sing a victory song with your spouse.

22

WHAT SHOULD I DO
WITH THESE SPIRITUAL TOOLS?

You now have the tools you need and should have already been working on using each one of them. You will be using some tools more frequently than others. Find out what works for you by testing each tool as different aspects pop up. By aspects, I mean that as you recognize Satan's various temptations and tactics, you will want to use different tools to thwart off his influence to separate you and your mate. You will begin to zero in on which tools work best for you. There is a simple procedure to remember when using these tools.

First, you must have the desire to change. You must have a strong desire in your heart to be better than you are. You must have the desire to help your mate be all they can be. You must desire to help them along as you are progressing. Have the desire to work together.

Second, you must make a commitment to work on improving yourself with these tools. Commit yourself on a course to perfection. Be persistent with this commitment. Never give up. Commit to your eternal mate to stay the course and fight a good fight against Satan's temptings and whisperings. Make a commitment to your mate to help them overcome their weaknesses as you overcome your own.

Third, you must make these tools part of your daily routine. You must practice them in your daily activities. Recognize what is happening. Recognize what you are feeling. Is it something that is negative or positive? Recognize the whisperings from Satan. Defend yourself and conquer your weaknesses. Once you recognize the negative situation, you can reach into this book and pull out something to combat that situation. You can pull out a tool that will help you remove the negative thought or feeling that you have. Maybe you have already said or done something that was negative and now you need a tool to correct it. Use the tool or tools you need to completely remove what needs to be removed. This will take some concentrated effort at first. After a while, your concentration and use of these tools will pay off by becoming a good habit. You will train yourself to automatically recognize that certain negative behavior or pattern you fall into. You will be able to correct it with ease. Next, after removing this negative thought, feeling or action, replace it with positive thoughts, feelings and or actions. Reinforce yourself and your spouse with positive actions so that the void left by removing negative things won't draw you back into the negative stuff you just got rid of.

Start With A Foundation And Build

It is like this. You start off with a flat piece of land that you want to build a house on. You want your home to be built upon a nice firm foundation don't you? So you dig trenches in the ground in order to pour the cement foundation, right? OK, what happens is that just as you dig the trenches, a rain storm comes and fills the trenches with water. Well, you can't pour your cement foundation until the water is removed because the cement would be too wet and wouldn't set right. You have to remove the water and dry out the ground. Then you pour the cement into the trenches and after it dries, you have a firm foundation from which to build your home. Once the home is built, it becomes a shelter from any other rain storms.

OK, what's that got to do with the spiritual tools in this book? Well, the land represents your life and the ground that is being prepared is the ground on which your marriage (the home) will be built. As in all marriages, there are challenges that we make for ourselves and challenges that we fall prey to with Satan's temptations. This is represented by the rain that comes down that fills the trenches that we have dug. We must get through these challenges in order to build a good marriage, represented by the home. The ditches that get filled up by the rain are our own minds. As trials in our marriage (the rain) fills up our minds (the trenches) with negative thoughts and feelings, this causes negative thoughts, feelings and or actions. When our trenches are filled with water, the first thing we need to do is recognize it is there. The sooner you recognize there is water in your ditch you need to do something about it. The best thing you could do is to recognize the negative thoughts when they come into your mind and stop them. Stop these negative thoughts in their tracks before they become a negative action or reaction. So, you get out *How To Build Marriage Unity That Will Endure Throughout All Eternity* and grab the tool or tools that you need and start pumping the water out of your ditches. Purge your mind of these negative and possibly satanic suggestions. Then, once the water is out of your ditches and the ground is dry again, pour the cement foundation for your home. Fill your mind up with positive thoughts about your spouse. Actually look for the positive things that you love about your mate. Think of thoughts that will fill up your ditches that will cement your relationship. If you get enough cement in your ditches, you will have a firm foundation on which to continue to build your marriage.

Each and every time that one of your ditches gets filled up with rain you will remember to follow this simple procedure. The funny thing is, as with building a home, eventually you will have enough foundation that your ditches will no longer fill up with rain. You will have all the cement in there that you need in order to repel the rain. The rain will no longer be a challenge. You will have learned how to recognize, remove and replace so fast that the challenges of the past will be no challenge at all. This is the goal that every celestial couple should strive for.

Is it achievable? I know with all my heart that it is certainly achievable. Many areas of my life have been changed for the better by just using these simple tools. I know you can do it too, if you want it bad enough. I have talked to many couples who simply do not believe that Linda and I have never had a fight or an argument. We have never had a fight or argument because we simply use the tools contained in this book. That's why we have put them all together and are sharing them with you. They have worked for us and I have been inspired of the Lord to write about them to help you. These tools are nothing new and have been around for use by anyone throughout the centuries. Many people have used them and have had happier lives because of it. We have simply put them down on paper for the use and benefit of all who read them.

We have found that so many people are just not aware of how to handle situations or even how they should treat their mates. This has always troubled me. At first it troubled me when I did not know about them. Now I am concerned for the welfare of others now that I do know about these tools. I am grateful to a Heavenly Father who has opened our eyes and given us such marvelous tools to help Linda and me to be the best eternal companions we can be.

WHO WILL BE THE BENEFACTOR?

As you master the use of these tools within the pages of this book, you will need to become aware of many things. One huge factor we have learned from using the tools contained here is that you will be more spiritually connected to our Heavenly Father. By doing so, you will be more susceptible to hear the promptings of the Holy Ghost. I have not talked that much about the good promptings you will hear along the path to a perfect celestial marriage. As you follow what is written in this book and truly strive to become a celestial couple, you will be prompted more and more by the good whisperings from the Holy Ghost to help you along the way. This is because you are striving to do what our Heavenly Father wants you to do. You are moving more on His side of the *football field of life* so to speak. You are getting closer to His goal line and thus being more under His influence and guidance. This is an individual thing as to how you are striving to live the commandments and having the desire to work on perfecting yourself.

As Linda said to me earlier, "I am working on improving myself. As I am working on improving myself I feel a tremendous difference in the way I feel. The whisperings of Satan are much less than they used to be and I feel the good whisperings enter my heart. This gives me peace that I have never felt before. Before, when I reacted negatively toward someone because of what they said to me I felt I needed to defend myself and felt angry inside. I felt they deserved what angry things I would say back to them. But when I started using the tools in *How To Build Marriage Unity That Will Endure Throughout All Eternity* I felt different. I thought as I used the tools that it would just be better for the other person. I thought that other people around me would benefit most from me not lashing out when I was *defending* myself. While that was certainly true, the big benefit became clear to me. I had never even dreamed that I could benefit too, but I have. I feel a peace that I have never felt before. Before, I would let my negative emotions get hooked to Satan's whisperings. When I would do this, I couldn't hear the whisperings from the Holy Ghost. The Holy Ghost's promptings were drowned out by all the negative emotion I was holding on to. I have now been able to disengage those negative feelings from Satan's whisperings. I have been able to hear the good whisperings and promptings from the Holy Ghost. The promptings from the Holy Ghost are much more prominent now. The peace and spiritual feeling inside me is so much more fantastic now than the way I used to feel." Wow, that just about says it all. Linda admits that Satan is still whispering and she still has to fight him off. She just has an easier time of it by persistently using the tools in this book.

THE TREASURE BOX

Something else you need to be aware of is that you are building a treasure box with the tools in *How To Build Marriage Unity That Will Endure Throughout All Eternity*. Yes indeed my friends, you need not look far to see your treasure box. As you and your mate use these tools, you will be filling your own treasure box with good things. These things will not be tangible things like you might find in a treasure box on an island somewhere. No, the treasure in this treasure box will be of more worth to you than all the treasure in the world.

Each of you is building up your own treasure box that is full of positive events in your life. It is filling up with enjoyable moments where you recognize how glorious your spouse is. It could be an outpouring of love that you felt from your mate when they overlooked your weaknesses. Added to the treasure box could be that changed heart as you forgave the other. A dose of appreciation may be flowing around inside the box. Truly, your spouse will become this treasure box as you work together to become the perfect celestial couple.

Treat your eternal mate like the treasure box that they are. Look at them and see the treasure right before your eyes. Value them and keep them safe in your heart. Appreciate them for all that they are worth, for they are worth plenty. Remember, you will take nothing out of this world that is of more value than your own soul. The next greatest thing that you will have in the next world is that of the companionship of your eternal mate. To me, that is a treasure and beyond.

Having your mate is like going to a treasure box and being able to access the finer things in life. You are rewarded by going there and finding love, compassion, patience, kindness, safety, and peace. Because you and your mate have used the tools to become a celestial couple, you each have treasure that you can give to one another. These are the kind of treasures that when you give them, you have more to give and you get more in return.

THE TREASURE BOX ASSIGNMENT

I want to give you one last assignment. Stop and get something to write with and a piece of paper. I want you to make a list of all the treasures in your eternal mates treasure box. Think of all the nice things you love about them. Write down what things they do that makes you happy and feel more secure. What is it that they do that makes you feel good and love to be around them. How have they made you feel at peace? What do you treasure most about them? What are their strong points that you admire? Write down all the ways that you noticed that they are improving on as you read this book together.

Once you are done with that list, make a copy of it and file it away somewhere that you will remember where it is in a year. In fact, put this date and location of the copy you wrote on your calendar, in your cell phone, computer or day timer. A year from now, I want you to do the same exercise again. Then go and get the paper you filled out today and compare them. I know as you both work on using the tools herein, you will find even more things to love about your mate. You will have a baseline from which to see improvement in your relationship. With the original, continue to update and revise as you go along over the next year. By keeping this in front of you and reading it on a daily or at minimum on a weekly basis, you will be confirming in your mind in a positive manner all the things you treasure about your mate. This will be a great reminder when the rain of difficulty beats against your marriage home of what a great treasure your mate really is. Focus your heart on that treasure and never let it go. This will keep your foundation strong as you press forward in life.

Keep on using these tools throughout your life. Don't just read this book once and put it down. There are so many great things within these pages that you will forget to use them from time to time. You must read this book many times and use these tools until they become habit. Even Linda and I read from this book each week to remind us of what we need to do. Keep these things fresh in your mind always. I promise that if you do this together and work at using these tools religiously, your life will change for the better and you will never want to go back to the way things were. You will experience a little heaven on earth as you become a great strength, a great strength together.

HELPFUL TOOLS IDENTIFIED
OR EXPLAINED IN THIS CHAPTER:

1. Find out what works for you by testing each tool as different aspects pop up.
2. Desire.
3. Commitment.

4. Use these tools in your daily routine.
5. Practice using these tools.
6. Recognize what is happening. Is it positive or negative?
7. Recognize what you are feeling.
8. Recognize the negative behavior or patterns you fall into.
9. Remove negative thoughts.
10. Replace the negative thoughts with positive ones. Fill your mind with positive thoughts about your mate.
11. Stop the negative thoughts before they become a negative action or reaction.
12. Use the tools in this book persistently.
13. Recognize how glorious your spouse is.
14. Treat your mate like the treasure box that they are.
15. Appreciate them.
16. Make a list of all the treasures in your eternal mates treasure box.
17. Keep this list handy so you can read it on a regular basis.
18. Read this book over and over again to keep the tools fresh in your mind.